NO PLACE ON THE C

No Place on the Corner

The Costs of Aggressive Policing

Jan Haldipur

NEW YORK UNIVERSITY PRESS

New York

NEW YORK UNIVERSITY PRESS
New York
www.nyupress.org

References to Internet websites (URLs) were accurate at the time of writing. Neither the author nor New York University Press is responsible for URLs that may have expired or changed since the manuscript was prepared.

Library of Congress Cataloging-in-Publication Data
Names: Haldipur, Jan, author.
Title: No place on the corner : the costs of aggressive policing / Jan Haldipur.
Description: New York : New York University Press, [2019] |
Includes bibliographical references and index.
Identifiers: LCCN 2018012213 | ISBN 9781479869084 (cl : alk. paper) |
ISBN 9781479888009 (pb : alk. paper)
Subjects: LCSH: Police-community relations—New York (State)—New
York. | Urban youth—New York (State)—New York—Social conditions. |
Immigrants—New York (State)—New York—Social conditions. | Community
development—New York (State)—New York. | Citizenship—New York
(State)—New York. | Crime prevention—New York (State)—New York.
Classification: LCC HV8148.N5 H35 2018 | DDC 363.2/3097471—dc23
LC record available at https://lccn.loc.gov/2018012213

For Anneka, Simon, Damien, and Maddox

CONTENTS

LIST OF FIGURES

Window air-conditioner units and fire escapes dot the red and tan brick apartment buildings on College Avenue, a street located just a few blocks east of the Grand Concourse in the southwest Bronx. Thursday afternoons in this area are often a very tense time for neighborhood residents. On what have become known as "Thirsty Thursdays,"[1] a weekly event in which officers from New York City's 44th Police Precinct flood the neighborhood in the department's trademark blue and white vans, young people from the community can disappear for hours and sometimes days at a time.

Young adults, primarily men but also women, in this and other neighborhoods in the South Bronx are transported in this vehicle to the nearest police precinct and held there until a family member can pick them up. The explanation for whisking away these young people is typically vague or even nonexistent—at best, sometimes nothing more than the comment that the youth was causing trouble or disturbing the peace. The crime prevention program under which these young people are rounded up and abruptly herded away is known as "stop, question, and frisk," or, colloquially, "stop and frisk."

In the early 2000s, New York City began to experience a surge in the use of this strategy, an aggressive police tactic that became a distinctive feature of the New York Police Department. Young black and Latino men disproportionately became the focus of this approach, which targets residents of selected neighborhoods throughout the five boroughs. Although the number of documented stops began to decline in 2012, aggressive policing has not disappeared and its impact continues to be felt by both the individual and the community.

This book draws from three years of intensive ethnographic fieldwork conducted before and after the landmark court decision *Floyd, et al. v. City of New York*, which was handed down by a federal judge in 2013 and ruled such stops unconstitutional. My research was conducted in and around the 40th, 42nd, and 44th Precincts in the western portion of the South Bronx, the latter of which was recently recognized by the *New York Times* as having one of the "highest use(s) of force" in the entire city. [2]

Relying primarily on participant observation, informal interviews, focus groups, and life-history interviews, this book examines how local residents make sense of aggressive policing tactics and explores the strategies and sources of resilience these individuals use to cope. I take a close look at residents' conception of what it means to be a citizen and how their right to public space has been transformed by aggressive policing tactics.

My findings suggest that this approach to policing has led to a substantial erosion of faith in local and state institutions. My research also shows that these aggressive policing tactics discourage the formation of social ties in the neighborhood, the very networks residents need to thrive and get ahead.

Aggressive policing, most visible through the department's highly publicized stop-and-frisk program, results in a number of negative consequences. Although high-profile cases of police misconduct often dominate the headlines, they are only a part of the story. Missed classes in school and missed shifts at work can put a strain on a young person's financial situation and are among the more visible collateral costs of this mode of policing. Less visible but also destructive is the severe emotional toll that results when members of the community are forced to make sense of the experience of growing up under surveillance.

With New York City widely hailed as a success story in its ability to reduce street crime and with other cities having begun to replicate the New York Police Department model, I believed it was essential to analyze the effects of aggressive policing strategies on communities in New York. Much of what we know about the impact of this form of policing comes from statisticians and policymakers, who are typically examining the issue from a distance. Using a more grounded ethnographic approach, I wanted to look more deeply at the unanticipated consequences of the use of this tactic to better understand how residents of the South Bronx, particularly young adults, make sense of policing in their community.

Much of the existing literature on policing and its impact on local communities focuses almost exclusively on justice-involved black and Latino individuals or, at the other extreme, recounts the stories of the community's highest achievers. By contrast, my goal was to expand on these narratives to gain a greater understanding of the effects of aggressive policing on the everyday lives of a broad range of local residents.

Specifically, I explore how different groups maintain a sense of community in the face of a looming police presence. I examine the ways that local residents remain resilient, along with the coping mechanisms and strategies they use to deal with this situation. I also examine the effects of this form of policing on residents' day-to-day lives—for example, how employment and education prospects may be affected. Perhaps most important, I examine residents' conception of what it means to be a citizen in such an environment and how the right to public space has been transformed by aggressive policing tactics.

In the Introduction, I begin by defining what aggressive policing means in New York City by focusing on the rise and subsequent decrease in the use of stop and frisk. I also provide a historical account of the role of the police in New York City communities, documenting the transformation of police practices over the decades.

Chapter 1 examines the experiences of the more achievement-oriented young people of the neighborhood, those "invisible youths" who may not be found out on the street, playing in the parks, or occupying other public spaces. These young adults have effectively been driven indoors through a combination of neighborhood violence and an aggressive police presence. In particular, I highlight the experiences of two groups of young adults in the neighborhood: "The Achievers," a group that often avoids creating community ties as a protective mechanism, and the "Line-Toers," those who try to reconcile community ties with their own personal aspirations.

In Chapter 2, I explore the experiences of young adults who have been involved with the court system and who often experience some of the harshest treatment from police. Subsequently, in Chapter 3, I discuss the experiences of local parents, who, although they are generally not the targets of aggressive policing, experience an acute form of trauma vicariously through their children. Many of these parents have developed a set of coping skills to help them deal with the emotional toll of having a son or daughter handcuffed and taken away and, on a more pragmatic level, to navigate the system when these situations occur.

In Chapter 4, I focus on the experiences of recent immigrants in the neighborhood, exploring how a lack of social capital coupled with the strength of ethnic group ties can provide a protective buffer between immigrant groups and police. Finally, in Chapter 5, I discuss the impact of aggressive policing on outcomes such as securing a conviction in court and offer some policy recommendations.

The impact of stop and frisk is of critical importance because of the dilemma inherent in aggressive policing in high-need communities. The very people who are typically victims of this approach are those who arguably need the most protection from the police. A humane and nuanced analysis of the implications and social and economic costs of this regime can only help policy makers address the issue with greater depth and understanding.

Introduction

I got a daughter. Luckily I don't got a son. But
what I think it does to little kids coming up—in
they mind it becomes regular. Like when they get
older, cops stopping them, they gonna remember
when they was little they always seen that. It's not
going to be out of the norm for them.

—Lance

In June 2011, I began spending time in the South Bronx,
where, as a graduate student in sociology at the Graduate Center of the City University of New York, I worked as
a research assistant for a local community-based research
project. It was around this time that media coverage of the
New York City Police Department's stop-and-frisk policy, an
approach in which police officers would stop and question
residents whose behavior struck them as "suspicious," began
to spike.

This was also the year that frisks, disproportionately effect-
ing black and Latino youth in low-income neighborhoods,
would reach their peak, with 685,724 stops documented, in a
city with a population of approximately 8.5 million residents.
Local newspapers such as the *New York Times*, *the Daily
News*, and the *New York Post*, as well as national publications

like the *Atlantic* and the *Wall Street Journal*, had begun covering the phenomenon, thus helping to shape a broader discussion of the subject.

New Yorkers seemed largely divided on the issue. For some residents, the city did indeed feel safer thanks to this approach—a stark contrast to the urban blight associated with parts of the city in the late 1980s and early 1990s. But at what cost, I wondered? The South Bronx neighborhoods in which I was spending time were experiencing some of highest frequencies of stops in New York City,[1] and I became curious as to how peoples' lives were shaped by this form of aggressive policing.

This curiosity served as the impetus to embark on this research project and begin spending time with local residents in and around parts of the 40th, 42nd, and 44th precincts of the South Bronx, which cover the Melrose, Morrisania, Highbridge, and Concourse Village neighborhoods. Some residents refer to the area as Morris, a reference to the avenue that bisects much of the borough's southwestern portion. But since the name is not in widespread use, and since neighborhood names in the Bronx can be tricky in any case, I refer to the area, which lies roughly west of Bruckner Boulevard and south of the Cross-Bronx Expressway, as the southwest Bronx or simply as the neighborhood.

Borrowing from the term made popular by the sociologist Robert K. Merton,[2] I sought to examine the so-called unanticipated consequences of Bloomberg-era stop-and-frisk policing. In areas like the South Bronx, aggressive policing creates yet another unneeded barrier to getting ahead. How,

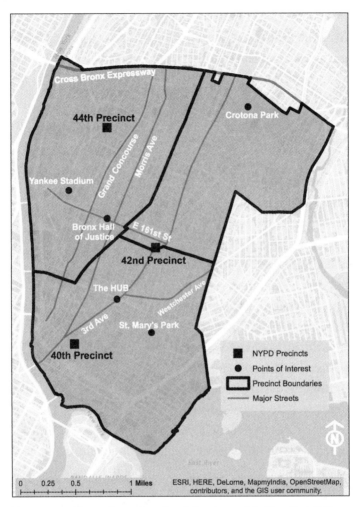

FIGURE 1.1. The 40th, 42nd, and 44th Precincts of the New York Police Department. Map courtesy of Will Shaw.

then, do families affected by this tactic manage? Are they able to maintain a sense of community? What is the impact of aggressive policing on residents' daily lives?

Due to the types of questions being asked, ethnography was the most appropriate approach to my fieldwork. This method is particularly useful when seeking to document the so-called lived experiences of members of such a neighborhood. These were questions that could not be answered in a survey or a brief interview on a college campus. I had to immerse myself in the community—spending time in residents' apartments or houses, at local gatherings, at pickup basketball games, on park benches, in bodegas, at court hearings, and at meetings with probation officers. And while I had a number of initial research questions in mind when I went into the field, I realized that many of these questions might shift over time. As part of a more "grounded" inductive approach, I was open to allowing my data to inform my hypotheses, as I spent more and more time in the community.[3]

Because of heightened attention from police, some residents were leery of outsiders in the community. For this reason, it was extremely important for me to spend time familiarizing myself with the neighborhood, and, even more important, for local residents to feel that they could trust me with their stories. Having lived and worked in the Kingsbridge section the Bronx for a time in my early twenties, I had some familiarity with the area. I often visited the neighborhood around Yankee Stadium, sometimes for a ball game but more often for a drink or to meet friends. Later on, I began mentoring high-school students as part of the Bronx

Brotherhood Project, at a local community center near where I began this research. In many ways, however, I was starting from scratch with this endeavor.

It wasn't until my teens that I began to more fully cultivate my own ideas about the police. Toward the end of middle school in Syracuse, New York, where I grew up, I began noticing how police officers can alter or interrupt people's lives, particularly the lives of young men of color. Although I grew up in a solidly middle-class household to immigrant parents from India and the Netherlands, my community did not always reflect my own circumstances. Syracuse, a mid-sized "Rust Belt" city, fell on hard times as I was coming of age in the 1980s and 1990s, as many of the factory jobs the city once depended on began to leave. In 2015, the *Atlantic* famously declared that Syracuse had the "highest rates of both black and Hispanic concentrations of poverty in the nation."[4] By the time I had graduated high school, a number of my peers had negative interactions with police, in some cases resulting in long-term prison sentences. To that end, particular moments still resonate with me and played a key role in my personal, and sometimes complicated, understanding of the police.

Despite my own sometimes negative experiences with law enforcement, I often shy away from being overly critical of the police. For every friend or acquaintance I've seen locked up, another has fallen victim to neighborhood violence, ostensibly underscoring the need for effective police work. It is at this critical juncture, the delicate balancing of community safety and fundamental human rights, where the primary dilemma lies.

In some respects, I came into this project selfishly seeking to make sense of what I had seen and experienced in my formative years. I sought to discover how others had themselves come to realize the role of police in their lives and, perhaps more important, how these experiences had shaped their trajectories. I was prepared to encounter a bevy of polarizing opinions, of which there were many.

I was unprepared, however, to discover how many people shared my complicated and occasionally contradictory attitudes toward the police. *It just wasn't that simple.* There were times when we shared a "fuck the police" attitude, and other moments when the presence of police brought a sense of calm and security. Moreover, although the criminal justice system is among the more visible prisms through which to view inequality in America, it represents only a small piece of the larger systems at play.

The Southwest Bronx

Many of the statistics typically used to describe communities such as the one I focus on do little justice to the human ecology of the neighborhood. Human, or "community" ecology, loosely defined, refers to the relationship involving people, their material conditions, and the physical space they inhabit.[5] Among some of the Ghanaian immigrants I spent time with, for example, the neighborhood is little more than a place to lay one's head, and consequently police harassment is often something of an afterthought. For others, like Glenda,[6] the neighborhood represents much more. It is a place to raise a family as well as a source of memories both fond and painful, the latter prompted largely by her teenage son's recent interactions with local law enforcement officials. Simply put, the neighborhood means different things to different people.

In many respects, the South Bronx of today is a far cry from the "Boogie Down"[7] of old. In the late 20th century, the area stood as a global symbol of urban blight, made infamous internationally by President Jimmy Carter's "walk down Charlotte Street" and by films such as *Fort Apache, the Bronx*.[8] Modern developments now stand where burnt-down buildings and decaying tenements once reigned. The neighborhood on which I focus is no exception, as it quite literally sits in the shadow of the recently renovated courthouse on 161st Street as well as the newly rebuilt, multibillion-dollar Yankee Stadium just blocks away.

Although in some respects this section of the Bronx is similar to many New York neighborhoods, a few important markers distinguish it from other communities. As academics such as the Harvard sociologist Mario Luis Small have cautioned, it is important not to cast poor urban neighborhoods as a monolith.[9] While parts of this neighborhood lack the desolate feel (as seen through a scarcity of stores and other businesses) that characterizes certain sections of Brownsville, Brooklyn, for example, it would be hard to compare 161st Street with more vibrant commercial districts such as 125th Street in Harlem or even Fordham Road to the north. Moreover, unlike a number of other high-need communities in New York City, the neighborhood is home to an

FIGURE I.2. 161st Street near the Bronx Hall of Justice. Photo courtesy of the author.

extremely diverse population, spurred on, in large part, by its growing immigrant base.

Perhaps the most influential transformation of Bronx life in the 20th century, however, came in the form of a seven-mile stretch of superhighway. Built over nearly three decades beginning in the late 1940s, the Cross-Bronx Expressway bulldozed its way through large swaths of the borough, disrupting and sometimes destroying entire neighborhoods. The highway quite literally divided the borough, cordoning off the South Bronx from the neighborhoods to the north.[10]

Around this same time, the labor market in New York City began to experience profound changes that would have a substantial impact on poorer neighborhoods. Although more closely associated with "Rust Belt" cities like Detroit, Buffalo, and Pittsburgh, rapid deindustrialization had a substantial impact on New York starting in the mid-20th century. Bronx residents, like their counterparts elsewhere in the city, could no longer depend on stable and well-paying union jobs to help support their families and ease them into the middle class.

This shift took a devastating toll on the South Bronx, one exacerbated by resistance by City Hall and other public and private entities to investing money or other resources in the area. The South Bronx, it seemed, was the subject of financial quarantine. Possibly for this reason, the area has largely been able to resist gentrification in a way that other neighborhoods with affordable rents and proximity to Midtown and Lower Manhattan have been unable to, such as the Clinton Hill/Fort Greene/Bedford-Stuyvesant sections of Brooklyn and Harlem in Manhattan.

For various reasons, the community has managed to maintain much of its black and Latino identity. As of 2010, approximately 46 percent of residents identify as black or African American, and 59 percent as Latino of any race.[11] In the early 20th century, the borough was a destination for Italian, Irish, and Jewish immigrants who sought to escape the relative chaos of Manhattan and make better lives for themselves and their children. Decades later, as white flight accelerated, black southerners and West Indians began settling in northern Manhattan and the Bronx.[12] Additionally, the Puerto Rican population of the Bronx experienced tremendous growth in the years following the passage of the Jones-Shafroth Act in 1917, which effectively granted Puerto

Ricans (a limited form of) American citizenship. Although there was steady growth in the Puerto Rican population in New York City in the years following this legislation, migration began to surge during the post–World War II boom.

In recent years, parts of the South Bronx have maintained a reputation as a destination for a wide variety of immigrant groups from around the world. The Concourse Village area in the 44th Precinct, for example, is among the city's fastest growing immigrant communities, with approximately 41,748 foreign-born residents, or nearly 41 percent of the area's total population.[13]

Each block, it seems, maintains its own distinctive character, with the sounds and smells varying depending on exactly where you are—even on which side of the block you stand. Walking down Morris Avenue, for example, one can see English slowly give way to Arabic signage on storefronts, only to shift again to Spanish-only advertisements for a party or other event. This is part of the cultural complexity of the Bronx, blending its rich Jewish, Italian, African American, and Puerto Rican histories with those of relative newcomers from countries like Ghana, Bangladesh, Guinea, and the Dominican Republic.

Near Yankee Stadium, on West 161st Street near River Avenue, one can find a number of bars, restaurants, and shops peddling Yankees-related gear. Passing Joyce Kilmer Park toward the Grand Concourse to the east, these businesses give way to a flurry of signs advertising legal services and bail bondsmen. The area is home to the New York State Division of Parole, the New York City Department of Probation, the

Bronx District Attorney's office, as well as a cluster of court-houses, the most visible being the Bronx Hall of Justice.

The huge, steel-framed structure, which opened in 2007 and sits a few blocks east of the Grand Concourse, occupies nearly two square blocks in the heart of the neighborhood. Although sought-after semipublic space is located near the rear of the building, the mere presence of the courthouse provides a constant and unsettling reminder of where one can end up.

Concourse Plaza, which is connected on one side to the Department of Probation, is the host of a Food Bazaar, one of the more prominent grocery stores in the area, as well as to a movie theater. Buildings in the rest of the plaza have begun to deteriorate, as clothing and electronics stores have gradually shut down, with signs advertising the promise of redevelopment prominently displayed over boarded-up doors.

For local residents, 161st Street serves as something of an informal dividing line. Directly to the south are several housing projects operated by the New York City Housing Authority, specifically Melrose Houses, Jackson Houses, and Morrisania Air Rights Houses. To the north are private apartment buildings and row houses. Most residents use the street as the landmark of choice when giving directions or describing a scene. In addition, many of the young adults I spent time with police their own movements according to their geography in relation to 161st Street, sometimes refusing to travel north or south of the boundary, depending on their orientation.

FIGURE 1.3. 138th Street in the 40th Precinct. Photo courtesy of the author.

Further south, parts of the 40th Precinct, in the southern-most part of the Bronx, have become something of a new fron-tier for real estate developers. In 2015, a sign near the Third Avenue Bridge proclaimed, much to the surprise of long-term residents, that the area was now the "Piano District," a desti-nation for "world-class dining, fashion, art, and architecture."

While this vision may still be a few years away, areas like the Hub, near 149th Street and Third Avenue, remain a vi-brant commercial district. The Hub, sometimes referred to as the "Times Square of the Bronx," has maintained an eclec-tic mix of retail chains and street vendors. Nonetheless, this part of the Bronx at times serves as a reminder of the bor-ough's gritty past. As recently as 2016, the *New York Times* began running a monthly series of articles titled "Murder in the 4-0," examining how homicide has persisted in the 40th Precinct, which encompasses the Hub, despite a downward trend of homicides citywide.

Historically, the South Bronx's 16th Congressional District, home to the western portion of the neighborhood, has been one of the poorest in the nation. In the Concourse Village section, where a number of the people I interviewed live, about 36.5 percent of residents live below the poverty line. This figure increases to 50.3 percent among those 18 and younger.[14] Fewer than 15 percent of residents (14.2%) age 25 or older have at least a bachelor's degree. To put these numbers in perspective, along affluent Central Park West in Manhattan, less than 20 minutes away, about 7 percent of residents fall below the poverty line while nearly 77 percent have at least a bachelor's degree.[15]

Sociologists such as William Julius Wilson regard communities like this as symbols of social isolation[16]—areas in which residential segregation effectively works to concentrate economic disadvantage.[17] Over the years, a number of sociological studies have focused attention on these communities. As many recent ethnographers have illustrated, in countless American communities the common denominator has been an intersecting web of blocked opportunities.[18] These exclusionary practices manifest themselves in myriad ways, although in 2018 the most visible form seems to be a criminal justice system that monitors and incarcerates poor blacks and Latinos at an alarming rate.

The New York Police Department

Since its founding in 1845, the New York Police Department has undergone a series of noteworthy transitions and ideological shifts. The department itself is divided into 77 precincts (12 of them in the Bronx) stretching across New York City's five boroughs and including specialized units such as the Transit Bureau, which focuses on the city's extensive mass transportation system, and the Housing Bureau, which polices New York City Housing Authority buildings. Some 36,000 officers hold a number of positions ranging from posts in the department's investigative units to administrative jobs at One Police Plaza, the department's headquarters in Lower Manhattan. During my research, approximately 42 percent of uniformed officers identified as black or Latino.[19]

Of course, the most visible arm of the New York Police Department is its patrol unit. This is typically the entry point for New York's police officers, and it is these men and women who often serve as the face of the department.

In the decades leading up to the increasing reliance on stop and frisk as a law-enforcement tactic, several important events transformed the department. The late 1960s and early 1970s were marked by corruption scandals culminating in the establishment, by Mayor John Lindsay, of the Knapp Commission, a task force that sought to implement a more rigorous system of checks and balances and to create a greater sense of accountability among officers.

By the mid-1970s, New York City found itself on the verge of bankruptcy. The city began to cut corners where it could, letting go of some recent Police Department hires and freezing any new hires. As the city began to rebound in the early 1980s, the department hired more than 12,000 new officers, many of whom did not undergo thorough background checks.[20]

In the early 1990s, yet another series of allegations of police misconduct ultimately led Mayor David Dinkins to create what was known as the Mollen Commission. Its findings revealed startling levels of brutality and exploitation. In the 75th Precinct in Brooklyn, for instance, police officer Michael Dowd and others were found to have committed crimes such as robbery and drug-dealing, with more senior officers often ignoring or failing to investigate allegations. As a 1993 article in the *New York Times* concluded, "The New York City Police Department had failed at every level to uproot corruption and had instead tolerated a culture that fostered misconduct and concealed lawlessness by police officers."[21]

As the public's faith in the Police Department continued to ebb, crime increased steadily in the 1980s through the early 1990s, the peak of the crack epidemic. In 1994, determined to rehabilitate the department's tarnished image, newly elected Mayor Rudolph Giuliani appointed William Bratton as police commissioner. After a stint as chief of the New York City Transit Police in the early 1990s, Bratton was selected to be commissioner of the Boston Police Department, only to be lured back to New York in 1994. Upon returning to the city, Bratton declared that "the entire culture of the New York City Police Department needed to be transformed."[22]

Mayor Giuliani's predecessor, David Dinkins, along with Police Commissioner Ray Kelly, had championed a "Safe

Streets, Safe City" program that emphasized community policing. Though appreciative of the infusion of new police force hires that accompanied this initiative, Bratton viewed their approach as largely ineffective.[23] As he wrote in his 1998 book, *Turnaround: How America's Top Cop Reversed the Crime Epidemic*, written with Peter Knobler:

> In theory, that's fine; beat cops are important in maintaining contact with the public and offering them a sense of security. They can identify the community's concerns and sometimes prevent crime simply by their visibility. Giving cops more individual power to make decisions is a good idea. But the community-policing plan as it was originally focused was not going to work because there was no focus on crime.
>
> The connection between having more cops on the street and the crime rate falling was implicit. There was no plan to deploy these officers in specifically hard-hit areas (to win political support for "Safe Streets," Dinkins had to commit to deploying cops throughout the city, in both low- and high-crime areas), and there was no concrete means by which they were supposed to address crime when they got there. They were simply supposed to go out on their beats and somehow improve their communities.[24]

As part of his response to the city's crime problems, Bratton implemented a multitiered approach designed to transform the police force. His focus was on getting illegal guns off the street, implementing a data-driven approach to policing, and renewing the focus on lower-level crime and social disorder. The highly publicized and frequently replicated "CompStat" (short for COMPuter STATistics/COMParative STATistics) system, developed by Bratton and Jack Maple, one of his chief lieutenants, was a management tool that used up-to-date crime statistics to help identify patterns and target areas for officers.

Perhaps most notably, Bratton implemented a form of what was known as broken-windows policing (also known as order maintenance policing or "OMP"), a strategy based on the idea that focusing on smaller quality-of-life offenses such as fare evasion ("turnstile jumping") and open-container violations (drinking alcohol in public) will lead to a decrease in more serious crimes.[25] This approach served as the ideological precursor to the stop-and-frisk policing that would define the next several decades.

As part of the metrics-driven policing ushered in by Bratton and Maple, the Police Department recorded street stops using a form known as the UF-250. This document, which has been slightly modified over the years, includes a range of data including personal information (name, age, gender, race), location and reason for the stop, and an indication of whether force was used during the encounter. Regardless of whether an arrest was made or a summons issued, UF-250s came to signify an officer's productivity in the field.[26]

It wasn't until 2003, however, that stop-and-frisk data became more publicly available. That year, the court decision *Daniels, et al. v. City of New York*, which alleged that department officers selectively targeted residents based on race, required the New York Police Department to provide quarterly data on stops—creating a level of transparency that would ultimately inform future cases.

In his 2005 memoir, *Blue Blood*, police officer Edward Conlon, who worked in and around the 40th, 42nd, and 44th Precincts of the South Bronx in the mid-1990s, praised some of the early effects of this policy that he witnessed after joining the force:

> The frequency of these "Stop and Frisk" encounters also changed the culture of how criminals carried their weapons: in the 1980's and early 1990's, many dealers would carry guns in their waistbands, and the decision to shoot someone—because he crossed into their territory, or he said something about their mother, or he looked at them funny, or just because—was a three-second decision. After Bratton, the dealers still had guns, but they were hidden under their beds or on rooftops, and the delay from impulse to act took five minutes or ten, allowing people to move and tempers to cool.[27]

Stop and frisk was beginning to capture the public imagination. Even after Bratton left the Police Department in 1996, the tactic was already deeply embedded there. Under Mayor Michael Bloomberg, Ray Kelly resumed his role as commissioner of the department in 2002 (in the early 1990s, he had enjoyed a two-year stint under Dinkins). Just months earlier, on September 11, 2001, New York City had been devastated by the terrorist attack on the World Trade Center. Upon assuming office, Kelly sought, among other things, to establish a Counterterrorism Bureau and incorporate counterterrorism training for all Police Department employees. This resulted in an increasingly militarized police force that was still committed to the principles of stop and frisk.

Under Kelly's watch, these stops escalated to a peak of 685,724 in 2011, and the public began to take notice. Pockets of resistance to the practice began to develop, and a vocal minority started voicing concerns about the racial disparities that defined this approach. Nevertheless, Kelly was unwavering in his support of the practice. "What bothered me," he wrote, "what still bothers me—is that the stop-and-frisk controversy managed to undermine a valuable, appropriate, and legal—let me emphasize *legal*—tool of modern law enforcement, one that had helped to save literally thousands of innocent lives."[28]

In November 2013, Bill de Blasio was elected mayor of New York. De Blasio, who had openly boasted about his politically activist past during his campaign, represented for many New Yorkers a welcome breath of fresh air, a radical departure from the bottom-line approach that became the hallmark of his predecessor, Michael Bloomberg.

One of de Blasio's first orders of business was appointing a new police chief to lead the nation's largest police force, fulfilling a promise he had based much of his campaign upon and one that, many hoped, would mark an end to the highly controversial practice of stop and frisk. In the end, as had happened nearly two decades earlier, William Bratton was ultimately chosen to succeed Ray Kelly.

This was a resounding "humility check" for many who were expecting the previous momentum against stop and frisk to continue. Starting in January 2013, Federal District Court judge Shira Scheindlin ruled on a series of cases involving New York City residents' right to public (and sometimes private) spaces. On January 8, in *Ligon v. City of New York*, Judge Scheindlin ordered the Police Department to immediately end the practice of unlawful trespass stops outside so-called Clean Halls[29] buildings in the Bronx. Operation Clean Halls allowed the Police Department to patrol private buildings throughout the city, and, in many cases, residents were subject to arrest in their own buildings if they did not present proper identification.

The most notable court decision came in August 2013, in the landmark *Floyd, et al. v. City of New York, et al.* case. Here, Scheindlin ruled that the rights of thousands of black and Latino New Yorkers had been violated by current stop-and-frisk tactics, calling for an independent monitor to be appointed. Around the same time, Scheindlin also granted the *Davis v. City of New York* case what is known as class-action status, thus allowing other cases to be included and become so-called class members in the lawsuit, which challenged the use of discriminatory stops in Housing Authority buildings.

Many of these milestone decisions coincided with and were perhaps motivated, at least in part, by a series of horrific events involving New York City residents and the police force. In 1999, the murder by police of Amadou Diallo, an unarmed 22-year-old Guinean immigrant, in the Soundview section of the Bronx, sparked significant media attention and would later prove to be the impetus for the *Daniels* lawsuit. Seven years later, in 2006, the death of 23-year-old Sean Bell, an African-American Queens native, struck a similar chord.

The murders of two New York teenagers, Ramarley Graham in 2012 and Kimani Gray in 2013, provide still more recent examples of the sharp disconnect between police and communities of color. Graham's case was particularly startling as he was murdered in his family's Bronx apartment, unarmed, at the age of 18. Officer Richard Haste, who was charged with manslaughter, was ultimately acquitted of all charges.

In the summer of 2014, just a few months into Bratton's tenure, the death of Staten Island resident Eric Garner led to a universal rallying cry for the transformation of policing in New York City. Garner, 43, was suspected of selling loose cigarettes, or "loosies," in the street. When confronted by the Police Department, one of the officers put him in a chokehold.

Garner repeatedly told the officers "I can't breathe" before losing consciousness. He was pronounced dead later that day, and the entire episode was caught on film that went viral instantly. A few months later, in December, a grand jury declined to indict the officer who had imposed the chokehold. This proved to be a tipping point as thousands of protesters took to the streets in New York City and beyond. "Black Lives Matter"[30] became a rallying cry, drawing national attention not only to the Garner case but also to the larger issues surrounding the deep-seated mistrust between police and minority communities.

Unequal Policing

Recent data suggest that the 40th, 42nd, and 44th Precincts of the Bronx, and New York City on the whole, have become safer in recent years. In his 2006 book, *Downsizing Prisons: How to Reduce Crime and End Mass Incarceration*, the sociologist and former New York City corrections commissioner Michael Jacobson cites New York as one of the first cities that, counter to national trends, effectively decreased prison use while simultaneously lowering the crime rate. The Police Department's CompStat data support this claim. In the 44th Precinct, for instance, offenses such as burglary and rape have decreased, reportedly by more than 40 percent each between 2001 and 2015, and the murder rate has decreased by 64.5 percent during this period.[31] The aggressive use of "stop, question, and frisk" in communities deemed "high crime" was mandated by several directives issued by the NYPD from the mid-to-late 1990s through roughly 2014. Yet departmental statistics gathered over the last 20 years confirm that assessments of suspicious behavior are highly discretionary and prone to a considerable margin of error.[32] In New York State, a 1964 piece of legislation (Code Crim. Pro. 180-a) gave law enforcement the authority to "stop, question, and frisk" an individual without a warrant based solely upon "reasonable suspicion" that he or she has committed or might be in the process of committing a crime. This statute marked a notable change from prior legal standards[33] that required officers to have a higher level of proof of potential criminality (probable cause) before stopping a member of the public.[34]

In 1968, along with its landmark decision in *Terry v. Ohio*,[35] the United States Supreme Court considered two New York City cases arising under this legislation. In *Sibron v. New York*, the Court ruled in favor of the defendant, and against the validity of an NYPD officer's use of "stop, question, and frisk." In *Peters v. New York*, the Court ruled in favor of the state—affirming the officer's right to stop the defendant based on a reasonable suspicion that he was involved in criminal behavior. The *Terry* decision validated "reasonable suspicion" stops as an acceptable police practice across the nation. At the time the New York legislation passed, and in a powerful dissent to *Terry v. Ohio*, civil libertarians and defense attorneys expressed concerns about how this expanded police authority might be used.[36]

Scholars like Bernard Harcourt and Tracey Meares[37] note that due to the socioeconomic and racial discrimination that often accompanies this type of discretion, the costs of policing are unequally distributed throughout society. African American adolescent males from economically disadvantaged areas, in particular, often feel targeted by police regardless of their involvement in delinquent behavior.[38]

To help explain why this happens, some psychologists point to a phenomenon known as "implicit bias," whereby unconscious attitudes and stereotypes permeate one's actions. Put simply, officers who may not be overtly racist may still hold subconscious racial biases, which in turn affect who they decide to stop. For young black and Latino men in the southwest Bronx, this means there is often a presumption of guilt. Moreover, America continues to be intentional with its policies that have, in no uncertain terms, targeted particular groups. This is not a new phenomenon. Rather, this history of criminalizing race, as noted scholars such as Michele Alexander,[39] Khalil Muhammad,[40] and more recently, Paul Butler,[41] have illustrated, can be traced back centuries.

In a study published in 2007, Andrew Gelman, Jeffrey Fagan, and Alex Kiss found that black and Latino New Yorkers were disproportionately stopped and frisked, and "more frequently than whites, even after controlling for precinct variability and race-specific estimates of crime participation."[42] The study also showed that among blacks and Latinos, these stops were actually less likely to lead to arrest than with whites.

Data from the Police Department's Stop, Question and Frisk Report Database, which is available to the public, demonstrate steady increases in documented stop and frisks in the 2000s. Yet only a small fraction of these stops (less than 12% in most years) resulted in a summons or an arrest.[43] For those arrested or issued a summons in the Bronx, the problems were likely just beginning. The borough has developed an unsavory reputation as having a tremendous backlog of cases, resulting in sometimes excruciatingly long court delays. People accused of lower-level offenses often spend a considerable amount of time making arrangements for tending to work and family responsibilities in order to attend court proceedings, only to have the case postponed to another date.

For those accused of higher-level offenses, the situation gets worse. In 2013, when this research took place, the Bronx led the city in having the most felony cases pending for two years or more. For those who were denied or could not afford bail, this translates to their being detained on Rikers Island, New York City's jail, until their court date, which in some cases could be years away.[44] The human cost of an inefficient court system is vividly demonstrated by the travails of a young Bronx resident named Kalief Browder. Browder was arrested at the age of 16 and detained for more than two years, much of which was spent in solitary confinement, on robbery charges that were ultimately dismissed. In 2015, a few years after his release, unable to escape the trauma of his incarceration, Browder committed suicide.[45]

In 2007, there were a reported 472,096 stops in the city. By 2011, stops increased to a peak of 685,724. In 2015, stops declined to 22,565, due largely to the 2013 *Floyd v. New York* decision. Yet even as documented frisks began to decline to presurge numbers, the crime rate continued to decrease. In 2011, for instance, a year marked by a historically high number of stops, there were 515 murders citywide. In 2015, that number had dipped to 352, thus seemingly bolstering the argument against the overuse of the tactic (see table on the following page). Still, the impact of these stops is still felt on both the individual and community level. Those stopped over this period were overwhelmingly male and predominantly people of color; in 2015, approximately 83 percent of those stopped identified as either black or Latino.

Politicians continue to place a substantial amount of the responsibility for crime reduction on street-level policing. Yet, for so many, the decrease in crime does not necessarily

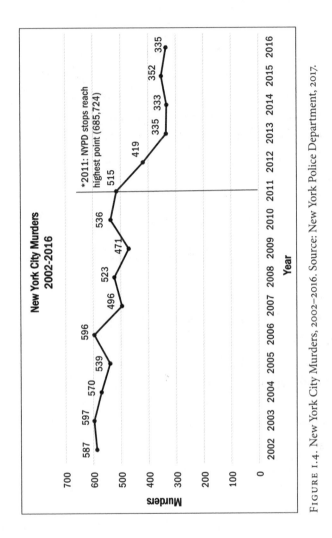

FIGURE I.4. New York City Murders, 2002–2016. Source: New York Police Department, 2017.

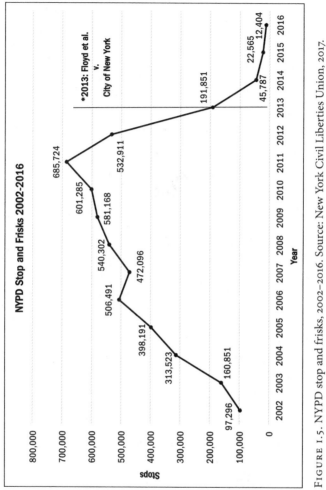

FIGURE 1.5. NYPD stop and frisks, 2002–2016. Source: New York Civil Liberties Union, 2017.

translate to greater community safety. Rather, in many cases, police have done nothing more than add an additional layer of community *in*security, with the effects often lasting far longer than the actual encounter.[46]

In the southwest Bronx, it is easy to see how pervasive and influential the criminal justice system has been for its residents. For countless young people in the neighborhood, negative encounters with the police have become a rite of passage. To borrow from the words of the eminent sociologist Max Weber, the aggressive policing tactics adopted by the New York police are yet another form of the state's "monopoly of the legitimate use of physical force within a given territory."[47]

The current system is seen as one which works to "manage" those on the "margins" of society—in other words, the poor, immigrants, single mothers, stigmatized minority groups, and the formerly incarcerated.[48] While what the sociologist Elijah Anderson[49] described as more "street-oriented" youth often become intimately acquainted with the criminal justice system at an early age, other local residents remain fully outside of its realm. This is no accident. Rather, as my findings suggest, many residents have developed a keen, localized sense of how to navigate their everyday lives in the face of aggressive policing tactics.

Neighborhood Effects

On the ground, scholars like Mary Patillo, David Weiman, and Bruce Western argue for a more holistic understanding of the criminal justice system and its effects on family and the community.[50] Beyond mere latent consequences of mass incarceration, the criminologist Todd Clear urges us to understand mass incarceration as having a profound impact on what he describes as "destabilizing communities."[51] Specifically, he seeks to look beyond the consequences for the individual to explore the impact for the community—tearing families apart, eroding the community's economic strength, and weakening informal social control mechanisms.

In her 10-plus years of fieldwork in the Bronx, the journalist Adrian Nicole LeBlanc illustrated many of the deleterious effects incarceration can have on a family over generations as the revolving doors of jail and prison dramatically alter the relationships and bonds created with both family and friends.[52] In this book, I argue that aggressive policing, regardless of whether it results in incarceration, can have a similarly transformative effect.

As men and women born in the early to mid-1990s, many of the young adults I spent time with find that they have inherited the devastation of the "crack generation." They are the daughters, sons, nieces, and nephews of a generation that, in large part, was systematically removed from society as part of the "War on Drugs" that defined the years under Presidents Ronald Reagan, George H. W. Bush, and Bill Clinton.

While this crusade had limited effects on crime, it effectively worked to incarcerate a disproportionate number of young black men in inner-city communities across America.[53] As the sociologist Bruce Western puts it, "Young minority men with little education bore the brunt of deindustrialization in the inner cities and experienced the largest increases in incarceration."[54] Further illustrating this phenomenon, a Pew report famously declared that 1 in every 36 Latino men 18 and older, and 1 in 9 African-American males between 20 and 34, are currently behind bars.[55]

For the young men and women on College Avenue, this often translated to the loss of a father, uncle, neighbor, or friend to the criminal justice system. And while many of these young people have not and likely will never experience long-term incarceration, as members of the previous generation did, they are all too familiar with its consequences. Herein lies a primary distinction. While past generations experienced the ill effects of mass incarceration, present-day black and Latino youth in New York City are subject to a form of widespread harassment. While this is considered progress in some circles, as many of these police interactions result in nothing more than a ticket, the aggregate effect of this form of aggressive policing can be just as insidious.

Searching for a Place to Stand

For young adults in the southwest Bronx, there is a pronounced shortage of places in the area to socialize or pass time. Local residents, particularly young men, are losing their right to the city.[56] The public parks, stoops, streets, and corners once emphasized by social scientists as spaces to congregate and create meaningful associations are no longer available to members of the community.[57]

Nowhere is this issue more critical than in a place like New York City, where space is at a premium. In densely developed neighborhoods in which a person can easily go stir-crazy in a cramped apartment during the hot summer months, New Yorkers increasingly rely on these public spaces as an escape. Yet instead of allowing residents in areas like the southwest Bronx to enjoy nearby public areas, an increased police presence has only helped deepen the wedges between local residents, thus hastening neighborhood disintegration. Perhaps more than any individual horror story or tale of distress, this is the most devastating, and most enduring, effect of the Police Department's pervasive use of stop-and-frisk tactics.

Among other negative outcomes, stop and frisk has also helped to intensify a greater culture of mistrust among residents of a "system" they have grown weary of. This has very real consequences, as local residents are far less likely to comply with a police force they view as unjust and not having their best interests in mind. Although a somewhat unorthodox source, I found a particularly telling excerpt in *Decoded*, the 2010 memoir of the music mogul Jay-Z, in which the rapper speaks to a weariness experienced by so many on the margins:

> Poor people in general have a twisted relationship with the government. We're aware of the government from the time

we're born. We live in government-funded housing and work government jobs. We have family and friends spending time in the ultimate public housing, prison. We grow up knowing people who pay for everything with little plastic cards—Medicare cards for checkups, EBT [Electronic Benefit Transfer] cards for food. We know what AFDC and WIC stand for and we stand for hours waiting for bricks of government cheese. The first and fifteenth of each month are times of peak economic activity.

We get to know all kinds of government agencies not because of civics class, but because they actually visit our houses and sit up on our couches asking questions. From the time we're small children we go to public schools that tell us all we need to know about what the government thinks of us.[58]

For a disproportionate number of young adults in the neighborhood, police are one of the first ways they are introduced to the government. As Michael Lipsky notes in his seminal work, *Street-Level Bureaucracy: Dilemmas of the Individual in Public Services*, "Most citizens encounter government (if they encounter it at all) not through letters to congressmen or by attendance at school board meetings but through their teachers and their children's teachers and through the policeman on the corner or in the patrol car."[59] Acting as an extension of the state, he continues, police are expected to "convey expectations [about] behavior and authority."[60]

How does this translate to neighborhood residents who are continually stopped for no other reason than the color of their skin and the neighborhood they live in? As I shall show, this form of aggressive policing affects one's sense of agency, eroding faith in both local and state institutions. Moreover, this policing regime actively discourages the formation of social ties in the neighborhood—the very networks often needed to get ahead.

A Note on Methodology

In working on *No Place on the Corner*, I was able to develop relationships and build rapport with four primary groups: achievement-oriented young adults, young adults involved in the criminal justice system, local parents, and recent immigrants (1.5 and second generation included). I settled on these delineations after spending extensive time in the neighborhood. Although it is an imperfect classification system in some respects, these became the most logical subgroups for my analysis. Still, seeing as we all occupy different roles in our day-to-day lives, these distinctions were far from "clean." For instance, some of my contacts who were recent immigrants also may have been justice-involved or achievement-oriented, or both. They were consequently grouped by which identity I felt trumped the others and was most useful for my analysis.

While these categories do not fully embrace the rich diversity of the neighborhood, each group contributes to a better understanding of both the shared and divergent experiences of people living in the area, capturing the everyday realities of a cross-section of the community across race, gender, age, socioeconomic status, and immigration status. Sensationalized accounts of poor neighborhoods often fixate on the lives of those involved in underground economies like the drug trade, making it easy to conclude that these neighborhoods are nothing more than penal colonies. Spending even a little time in the southwest Bronx, it becomes clear that this couldn't be further from the truth. During my fieldwork, I spent time with a number of young men who are involved in the criminal justice system. But while these young men are certainly a part of the human ecology of the neighborhood, they are also, in many ways, outliers. Most of the people I met are hard-working men and women trying to get ahead and make better lives for themselves. Due to their busy schedules—juggling work, school, and other appointments—they often become less visible in the neighborhood. Moreover, as my findings support, these residents are often driven further indoors due to neighborhood conflict and an overactive police force. Although they are probably less likely to be found socializing by the bodega on a Saturday afternoon, they are still an integral part of the community's story.

I began exploring this subject with only a rough idea of which people I wanted to include in my analysis. Over time, the subgroups mentioned began to materialize, and I found myself zigzagging across the 40th, 42nd, and 44th precincts. Because this project took on the form of a somewhat comparative ethnography, my geography in the neighborhood often felt scattered. Different groups spent time in different areas. When spending time with some of the more "achievement-oriented" young adults, I might visit the after-school college-preparatory center or shoot hoops at the Big Apple summer league. In the case of some of the young adults involved in the criminal justice system, I might meet them at a probation check-in or just hang out with them at their apartment. In all cases, the things we did and the space we occupied varied greatly depending on the individual. This ultimately contributed a great deal to my analysis, as I was given additional insight into how people's pieces of the neighborhood were reshaped by police tactics.

Moreover, as I soon discovered, my relationships with certain community members often precluded me from associating with other residents. Most notably, my ties with area mothers and fathers occasionally prevented me from talking to *their* children. While strict confidentiality was preserved throughout the study, some young people were still cautious of the hypothetical risk that information could be shared with their parents. Although this initially frustrated me, I came to empathize with the young adults. After all, what teen really wants to run the risk of their mother and father knowing their business?

In doing ethnography, you often are allowed into people's "backstage"[61]—the parts of their lives that the rest of the world may not ordinarily get to see. While this often provides for rich ethnographic data, folks occasionally take issue with how parts of their stories are represented. This is perhaps one of the greatest challenges of doing ethnography, but, unfortunately, it is one that is unavoidable. Given the topic of this book, I took particular care to change any identifying information in order to preserve the anonymity of those involved. Names, some locations, and other personal information were altered for the sake of privacy, although I went to great lengths to keep the character of the community intact. I am deeply thankful to the men and women whose stories fill these pages, who after a long shift at work, or lengthy exam, would find time to meet with me, even when it was the *last* thing on their mind. Without their participation and commitment, this project would not exist.

1

The Invisible

I don't want this following me around, you know?
It's like they got my picture and fingerprints now.
For what? They took them when they brought me
in the precinct. I don't want it to follow me like a
stigma or whatever. I hate knowing it's there and
could mess my whole life up. I'm not no criminal.
—Los

On a cool June morning, I arrived on 161st Street in the
Bronx. My watch showed 8:15 a.m. as I exited the subway
turnstile, still groggy from waking up at 6:00 in the morning
and making the trek from the Bedford-Stuyvesant section of
Brooklyn. The usually busy thoroughfare was much calmer
than it is when games are being played at the ballpark just
down the hill. Yankee Stadium was closed save for a handful
of security guards manning the perimeter.

As I neared the Bronx Hall of Justice courthouse, on 161st
Street and Morris Avenue, I could see a line beginning to
form between two steel dividers, with people waiting either
alone or in pairs. The line was filled with black and Latino
faces, and the group was overwhelmingly male, although
a handful of women were scattered about, many of whom
seemed to be the partners of those waiting in line.

The courthouse is a modern, multilevel glass building with a new outdoor cement atrium toward the back. Armed officers in uniform monitored the line. About 40 people were already waiting to enter when I arrived, but because the building's main doors were not yet open, the line was not moving. Within minutes of my arrival, however, the line began to grow quickly. A loud Puerto Rican man could be heard talking to a black man behind him; they did not seem to know each other but appeared to be swapping stories. Many of the faces looked anxious, and justifiably so.

Across the street, the Concourse Plaza shopping center looked almost entirely empty, devoid of cars and people. The few stores that were not boarded up for good had yet to open for the day. At about 8:30, the front doors to the courthouse opened up and those waiting in line began to file in.

* * *

Los texted me to let me know he was on his way. I anticipated he would bring a member of his family, but when he showed up, a shade after 8:40, he was alone.

Los is a dark-skinned Dominican male in his early 20s. He wears glasses and has an athletic build, with neatly cropped hair faded into a small Afro. He arrived to the courthouse wearing a pair of green army fatigues, T-shirt, a gray hoodie, and black and green Nike Air Penny shoes on his feet. As we waited to pass through the metal detectors, he apologized for his tardiness and looked visibly nervous. This was hardly surprising.

Today was Los's long-awaited court date for an incident that had taken place six months earlier, in January 2013, near his grandmother's apartment, a few blocks north of Yankee Stadium in the 44th Precinct. In addition to working full-time at a major department store in Manhattan, Los is a full-time student at a community college in Queens. It was on a break between classes that he decided to stop by his grandmother's place.

Although Los lives with his mother and sisters in the nearby Morrisania Air Rights Houses, a public housing complex, he often stops by his grandmother's home to check up on her. Near her building, he was stopped by police for the first time:

> They patted me down and they actually found my pocketknife. In order for them not to injure themselves, I told them that there was a pocketknife in there. It wasn't taken out, it was actually folded. I noticed that I had my knife that day, but, on January 1st it was New Year's. I was working the whole day. I had a 12-hour shift from 8 a.m. to 8 p.m.
>
> I was working with my knife [a blade used to open boxes in the stockroom] the whole day. It's something that I always leave at home. I don't carry it with me in public, I don't take it anywhere because I don't want to get stopped and all that. That day I intended, well I actually didn't intend at all, I just forgot to leave my working knife at work. It was no intent for me to take it out in public to show off or nothing like that. On Thursday, I happened to have the same sweater in which I worked on January 1st. That's how the cops got me with the

knife. I was arrested. They actually charged me with possession of a weapon in the 4th degree, in which . . . the cop
actually gave me a DAT, which is a "Desk Administrative
Ticket" [Desk Appearance Ticket] in which I have to see a
judge and confess my crime, to see what I plea.

Despite Los having a spotless record and insisting multiple
times that his "weapon" was in fact a work knife, the police
continued to process Los's arrest. Shocked and embarrassed,
he called me the day after he was released from the precinct.
A few days later, I walked him over to the nearby office of the
Bronx Defenders, a community-based organization that provides legal help for Bronx residents. As we walked down Court-
landt Avenue, toward his mother's apartment, Los, who usually
seems jovial and carefree, was sullen and withdrawn. He said:

Right now, I'm feeling like the criminal justice system is
viewing me as a criminal. I'm not a—first of all, this is my
first offense. I've never been arrested in my life before. I don't
think I should be treated this way because I'm actually study-
ing criminal justice and it's something that I love—and just
because I forgot to leave my working utensils at work, I'm
now being viewed as a criminal. It's something that I don't
actually like to be viewed as, by the society or public. That's
not the kind of person I am. I don't hurt people. I don't rob
people—I'm just not that kind of person.

In his seminal 2000 work, *Code of the Street: Decency,
Violence, and the Moral Life of the Inner City*, the sociologist

Elijah Anderson makes a distinction between "decent" and more "street-oriented" residents in a Philadelphia neighborhood.[1] Although no one truly falls neatly into a single category, it's clear that Los aligns himself more with the former group. Still, many residents must endure a DuBoisian "double consciousness"[2] that involves at least two primary categories: the way many of the young people in the community categorize themselves and the way others, namely the police, do.

In this chapter, I will focus on the experiences of those who fall on the more "decent" end of the spectrum. Because this group is by no means a monolith, I shall seek to reflect the rich diversity of their experiences. Their active schedules, combined with an aggressive police presence and conflicts in the neighborhood, often preclude these residents from frequently socializing in public spaces. Thus, to outsiders, they are largely invisible. These are the young men and women that I've identified as achievement-oriented, both in terms of the way they define themselves and by their actions.

The young people discussed in this chapter do not have a criminal history. They were typically enrolled full time in high school or college, or were working toward this goal. Or they had a job or were looking for one. It is important to separate so-called decent youths from so-called street youths, because the mechanisms used to make sense of and cope with police surveillance differ greatly among the two. Furthermore, many of the policy implications diverge in a similar manner.

FIGURE 1.1. Two boys play basketball using a makeshift hoop. Photo courtesy of the author.

During the first 20 years of Los's life, he was able to remain out of the reaches of police in a highly monitored neighborhood.[3] While many people have been able to avoid police contact in a similar manner, countless other "decent" young men were less fortunate. I met Octavius, or Tae, as he likes to be called, while playing basketball over the summer at a local junior high in the 44th Precinct, a site for the Big Apple Games.[4] Tae, who is 18, is a tall and wiry light-skinned African-American male who prides himself on his basketball prowess. He lives up the street from the school with his grandparents. Although he dropped out of school when he was 16, he is currently attempting to get his general education degree (GED) while working part-time at a Target near his mother's apartment in New Jersey.

Unlike Los, Tae had his first contact with police when he was in elementary school. "[I was] eight when I first got stopped," he told me. "It was like five of us and they thought we was throwing rocks off the roof because someone was complaining. It wasn't us, though." According to Tae, such interactions became much more frequent in his teens. "Thirteen, 14, that's when I get stopped at least three times a week," he said. "Even if it's not around my block, if I'm going to walk somewhere, I'm always getting stopped."

Stories like Tae's show just how common this type of police interaction can become for young men in places like the southwest Bronx. For some, police interaction in the early teens has become a rite of passage. Yet others who live in the same neighborhoods and attend the same schools remain largely out of the reaches of local officers. Why is this? How can we account for the different experiences of Tae and Los?

Is It the Shoes?

The excitement is palpable in Tae's voice as he describes the newly released "South Beach LeBron's." Priced at a hefty $250 ($200 if you "got the hookup"), the sneaker is the ninth edition of National Basketball Association player LeBron James's famed line, and the first to be released in pink, teal green, and gray—homage to the unofficial colors of the city of Miami, where James was playing at the time. At length, Tae explains to me what sets these shoes apart from the others, and regretfully explains that they sold out before he was able to purchase a pair. His disappointment is short-lived, as he then tells me excitedly about his newly discovered inside connection at House of Hoops, an athletic shoe retailer, which could aid in him getting a pair of "Foams" (Nike Air Foamposites, priced at $250).

I was 27 when I began this research project, still not far removed from my days as a "sneaker head." Growing up, sneakers were a form of currency for me and my friends. To have a pair of Nike Air Jordans even just a few days before their official release date signified an increase, however brief, in one's social status; to have a pair of "exclusives," or hard-to-find sneakers, meant something even more. Regardless of where you came from or how much money you made, sneakers, in their own distorted way, were the great equalizer. How you dressed, and especially what you wore on your feet, could counteract nearly everything else about you.

The so-called sneaker culture is alive and well in the Bronx, as it is in most urban and increasingly suburban centers around the country. This is not a new phenomenon, however, and it is well documented as a form of personal expression.[5] Young adults meticulously construct outfits from the ground up, coordinating sneakers with pants, tops, hats, and even belts. For some, the imperative is simply to match— green with green, brown with brown, and so on. For others, the goal is to set themselves apart, wearing more flamboyant color schemes, hard-to-find "vintage" pieces, or, in some cases, high-end brands.

Regardless, the common underlying factor is that most young people seem to understand the significance of presentation in how one is perceived by their peers and, increasingly, by the police. As a result, these young adults are forced to regulate and monitor their choice of clothing in ways that other Americans simply aren't.[6]

A number of young men and women I spoke with emphasized the importance of clothing in explaining their perceptions on why police did or did not elect to stop them. Many were acutely aware of how personal choice in dress could draw unwanted attention from the police. Choice in color, style of accessory (for example, a beaded necklace versus one that was silver or gold), or even the logo on a hat or a shirt are all subject to misinterpretation and can serve as an entry-point for police contact. As Louisa, a Puerto Rican high school junior, said of her brother's recent interaction with police:

> My brother—I guess it was the way he was dressed, I think. He was just stopped for no reason. I mean, I was there and I saw him from across the street and I asked him, and he was like, "Oh, he just stopped me." He was just walking because he was meeting up with me . . . and I guess it was just the way he was dressed.

Although this particular stop did not result in an arrest or a ticket, both she and her brother walked away angry and confused. Shelley, a classmate of Louisa, offered a more detailed attempt at an explanation. "It's the sagging—the hoodies—the big coats they wear now," she said. "Yeah, it's called a 'Biggie.'[7] It's like a big Merm . . . yeah, and it's, like, yellow, bright colors." In pockets of the South Bronx where there is greater perceived racial homogeneity, items like a "Biggie," hooded sweatshirts, beads, and sagging pants can provide sufficient "reasonable suspicion" for officers to stop black and Latino youth.

A number of the young women I spoke to gave poignant examples of how clothing affects how they are perceived by police. Suzanne, a Puerto Rican woman in her late teens, often wears clothing more closely associated with contemporary men's fashion. During summers, this consists of white T-shirts and shorts; come colder months, it's hoodies and jeans. As part of her personal style, her hair is neatly braided into cornrows and often covered by a fitted hat. She described an incident that occurred earlier in the summer in which her choice in clothing led to her being both inappropriately stopped and improperly identified as a man:

> I had this one time I was walking home when it was getting dark and these two officers jumped out on me and started asking me questions or whatever. This one officer asked me to turn around and started frisking me. I'm like, "You know I'm a girl, right?" I'm thinking, they think I'm a boy or something. So, he says, "Yeah, I know." And continues searching me! He didn't get a female officer or nothing.

Similarly, Tika, an African American high school senior in her late teens, recalls a recent time when she was frisked. In her opinion, the jean jacket she was wearing served as a trigger for the improper search of her and her friends:

> TIKA: Last year, summertime, I had a jean jacket on and when I dig in, I hold my jacket up [she put her hands in her pockets and lifted her arms in the air to demonstrate]. They jumped out—I was like—
>
> JAN: You were by yourself?
>
> TIKA: Me and my friends. Females. They was like, "Don't move!" I'm like, "Don't move? What you mean don't move? What I do? What did I do wrong?" "What you got in your hand?" [the officer said]. I let the female search me and then that was it. It's just like—and in the area I live in, cops ride through that block all day. All day. So, it's not really much they can do out there, but the cops take they jobs sometimes to the—it's too much.

Antwan, an 18-year-old African American high school senior, lived for several years in the Melrose Houses in the 40th Precinct, and more recently in the Alfred E. Smith Houses on Manhattan's Lower East Side. While he is acutely aware of others around him being harassed by police, namely his brother, he is quick to assert that he himself has never been frisked. As Antwan reports, "Well, I've seen people get stopped and frisked. In my experience, they mostly, they have their pants below their behinds with the hoodies and the fitted caps. They look sort of suspicious in a way, like they want to get stopped."

The Achievers

Antwan associates certain clothing with negative behavior, in a way justifying the attention from police officers. Although his school does not require uniforms, Antwan typically wears khakis and a button-down shirt, in his own way shielding himself from negative attention from the police. He further distances himself from situations and people he feels might compromise his personal safety and freedom by restricting the places where he hangs out and the people he interacts with. For many young people like Antwan, this results in a withdrawal from their community, and at times even from their family.

Whereas many of his peers socialize outside or at friends' houses after school, Antwan told me that he stays in school as late as he can, even spending lunchtime in the library to avoid potential conflict with classmates. His day begins at 6 a.m. and generally lasts until 5 p.m., "until school security kicks me out." After school, he goes to an after-school college-prep program located near the Grand Concourse, usually arriving home around 7.

While it would be convenient to attribute Antwan's withdrawal strictly to police harassment, the reality is a much more complicated algorithm that includes past negative experiences in the neighborhood and a history of changing residences:

> The Melrose Projects—I lived in there, where the son chopped up the mother, and there's other stuff that happens in that neighborhood. I never really felt safe. I would never

try and come home past a certain time or I would try and be inside at a certain time because I—for starters, I didn't know the neighborhood that well and I never felt safe.

I lived near Soundview for 10 years of my life. You see, I knew that neighborhood, so I knew where I could go and where I can't go. And then I started moving around and began to confine myself more and more. After about a certain age, I sort of disassociated myself with a lot of areas because I never felt safe. Most of the time I stayed indoors because when I tried going outside with the neighborhood children, the people—it was like I would always create enemies. So I just stopped coming outside.

During my fieldwork, I encountered a number of young men and women who told similar stories. Typically they were currently in school or college-bound, or both, and in many cases had managed to have almost no contact with the criminal justice system. But these "achievements" came at a steep social cost, as many members of this group were forced to loosen their ties to the community as a protective mechanism. In New York City, where teen social circles are often divided into "school friends" and "neighborhood friends," neighborhood friends are often the first to be cast aside.

Beyond that, many young people seemed to distance themselves from the physical landscape as well, avoiding community outings and gatherings. Those in this subgroup were often outwardly uncomfortable straddling both worlds: that of their school/professional world as well as that of the community. For those like Antwan, this presented too much of a risk. The decision to avoid contact with community members was not made in haste; rather, it was an informed decision based on years of experience. They are acutely aware of their vulnerability to police as well as to community violence, and so they reacted accordingly.

For many of the local achievers, the after-school center was one of the "safe spaces." In an area with a dearth of accessible and affordable (read: free) resources, the center was one of the few reliable spaces young adults could count on. It is housed on the ground floor of an apartment building on a side street near a busy thoroughfare in the borough's Highbridge section. Its computer lab is home to 10 computers, all of them occupied by students during after-school hours.

A staff of five full-time employees helps to keep the center afloat, organizing college visits, assisting with the college application process, FAFSA (Free Application for Federal Student Aid) forms, and in general demystifying the college application process. Young adults are typically referred to the center by local guidance counselors and by word of mouth. While new enrollees are welcome, the center is typically filled with familiar faces who, even after the college application process is complete, stop by to use the computers, socialize with friends, and talk with staff members.

One afternoon, I met with Antwan and two of his friends from the after-school center—Shep, an African American male, and Luis, a Puerto Rican male—both high school seniors at nearby institutions. Shep and Antwan are heading to State University of New York (SUNY) schools upstate. Luis plans to move in with his sister in Long Island. Our conversation ultimately settled on the issue of how these young men navigate their neighborhoods, and this exchange, involving Antwan, Shep, and me, was particularly telling as to how relationships with neighborhood peers are often managed:

ANTWAN: The friends I knew, that I grew up with—I know what they do with the drugs and some carry weapons. I just know I can't hang out with them because by chance, like there's a police station across from where we live, if they want to stop and frisk them, I might then get in trouble because I'm with them.

JAN: That's a great point—

ANTWAN: Yeah. When I was living here [in the Bronx] I knew people, right near my high school. Some people I knew I couldn't hang out with because I knew what they do, and I did not want to be, like, charged with any type of association . . . . I've never been stopped by cops and I don't want to start.

SHEP: Oh, definitely. I know a lot of people like that. People that aren't in my main group—like, first of all, I talk to a lot of people, right? People who I am likely not to, sort of, engage in a proper conversation with as friends, would typically be those people into that kind of lifestyle and in the case that I do talk to them, it would be a little bit like, "Oh, hey, 'sup?" You know what I mean? Just a "Hi, oh, hey, how are you doing? Did you pass this class? Fail this class?" Whatever. The topic usually goes to school and then I sort of cut the conversation and leave—on purpose, but not to make them seem, like, not to make

> it seem like I'm trying to avoid them. You know what I mean?
>
> ANTWAN: Yeah—with people who are about that life, they know what I am about, so they know, like, certain things I won't do. So they won't ask or try to come around me with certain things if they're doing something. Like, there were instances where they were gonna do something, but they'll tell me like, "Yo, you can't come along, we're doing something else, so just leave."

Antwan and Shep are aware of the importance of neighborhood-level ties. While they may sometimes want to avoid contact altogether, they realize this is impossible. Instead, they must "toe the line" with their social networks—in other words, establish enough of a connection so as to not seem dismissive or attract negative attention from other young men in the neighborhood, but at the same time maintain enough distance so they do not become embroiled in their friends' transgressions or become "guilty by association" in the eyes of the police.

For young adults in the southwest Bronx, this need to be constantly on guard can hinder their ability to get ahead—impeding access to employment and postsecondary educational opportunities. Previous work from the sociologists Philip Kasinitz and Jan Rosenberg has emphasized the challenges that urban dwellers often face finding employment, even when there are jobs to be found in their own backyard. As the authors note in their study, "Being a member of a stigmatized race, living in a stigmatized place, and not having a sufficient diversity of social connections all come together to block residents' access to jobs."[8]

Even when these social ties are realized, according to Sandra Susan Smith, a sociologist at the University of California at Berkeley, it is often challenging to "activate" these networks so they translate into actual work.[9] These barriers are compounded for young men like Antwan and Shep, who are, by and large, forced to forfeit their social ties in the community altogether as a means of protecting themselves from both the police and, at times, their peers.

Toeing the Line

It is an imperfect balance that many of the "achievers" have settled upon. They must sacrifice personal connections in an attempt to avoid negative attention from the police and community. By contrast, other young men and women I met were able to more effectively reconcile neighborhood ties with their own personal aspirations. In many cases, however, this came with a different type of social cost: increased contact with police.

One afternoon, Tae and I decided to meet at a local library on Morris Avenue. The drab brick building was typically a neutral, "drama free" space for residents, but over the past few years, it had become a site of increasing hostility between warring crews. This was due in part to its proximity to these groups—a central space within walking distance of both the

Melrose, Jackson, and Morrisania Air Rights public housing projects just south of 161st Street and the apartment houses that line the avenues further north.

Tae was running late, so I sat upon the white cement railing, trying to look inconspicuous as I scribbled a few notes on my iPhone. From my perch, it was hard to ignore the shadow of the huge glass courthouse directly to my left. I was interrupted by a heavyset black man in his early 30s, who told me, "You better be careful out here, my man."

"Why, what's up?" I asked.

"Some girl got shot right here in front of the building," he replied. "I don't know much about it, but check the news, it was all over the news." A few minutes later Tae arrived wearing a maroon American Eagle shirt with a matching hat and sunglasses. Grabbing a table in the basement, we began making small talk, although Tae seemed preoccupied. We discussed the dismal state of our beloved New York Knicks. Then he started to tell me about the feud that his block, near 166th Street and Sherman Avenue, is having with a crew near 164th Street.

Despite having bounced around quite a bit in recent years, most recently living at his aunt's house in New Jersey and the house of a childhood friend in Maryland, Tae remained loyal to a group of five friends from his childhood neighborhood, many of whom lived in the same building: "Two of them is playing [basketball] in college, the other is just in college, one of them died, and the other one . . . he like to smoke. I don't smoke, so . . . yeah . . . that's when we started breaking up."

Despite somewhat divergent paths, Tae, the youngest of the group, cites these friends as sources of resilience and motivation. He is the only member of the group not to have graduated from high school, apart from Sammy,[10] who was gunned down a year earlier, only a few months before graduation. Unlike Antwan and Shep, Tae maintains strong ties to other young adults in the neighborhood. He is a charismatic individual who seemingly knows how to, in his eyes, "toe the line" in the community. While he actively engages with other people who live in the neighborhood, he is not blind to the transgressions of some of his peers. "They know what I do, they know what I don't do," he said. "Like, 'I'll see y'all later, y'all do what y'all do. I'll go back around the corner, y'all call me when you done.'"

It is this very loyalty and unwillingness to compromise his ties to neighborhood friends, however, that has, in many cases, resulted in negative outcomes. Because of these associations, he at times "inherits" neighborhood conflicts, as is the case with the current dispute between his block and other local crews. Although he does not actively engage in the conflict, he realizes he must now reevaluate how he navigates his own neighborhood:

> TAE: There's a couple of blocks I try to stay away from now because there's stuff going on back and forth, like, two days ago somebody got shot in front of here [the library]. She got shot right out here. There are certain blocks. This is one of them.

JAN: This seems like an all right block, though.

TAE: This block—but the people that hang out around here, that live down the block in Emma's building.[11] We now have problems.

JAN: Your block does with them?

TAE: Yeah, so it's just—

JAN: But you're on Sherman?

TAE: Yeah, I'm on Sherman.

JAN: But that block is on Sherman too.

TAE: That's crazy. I know. We only like two blocks away. They was shooting back and forth—I'm across the street [from the school], but, down the block. They're on the other side, like right there. That's why I had to bring my shades because they shooting.

JAN: Just because you're from that block—

TAE: Yup. Just because I'm from there. "Yo, he from 66, right? Yeah." We all know each other because we all used to chill with each other. The day you met me at the Big Apple, we all be in there. I don't know what it's going to be like this year because I know ain't nobody stop beef from going to the Big Apple, but I still want to play ball and do all that—this summer is gonna be crazy.

JAN: So this is all recent?

TAE: Recent. Within the past two months is when all this happened. I don't even know what happened. I just walked outside one day, "Yo, we got beef with 1-6-4." For what? I don't know, but I can't walk down to 161 or nothing.

JAN: You don't even go down to 161—

TAE: If I do, I go all the way up to the Concourse, go across, and then come down—I don't walk on this path because that's where they be at.

JAN: So even if it doesn't directly involve you—

TAE: Yeah, I ain't got nothing to do with it, but at the same time you ain't gonna sit here and tell me, "You from here so I'ma do this and this." Like, all right, so we just gonna have to fight. So to avoid all that, if I don't have to come this way, I don't—but today I did. So instead of having to come all the way around because I was already late, I just took it straight down Morris.

JAN: So how does that affect you going to work? That makes you go a whole different route now.

TAE: Yeah, there's a lot of places where I just don't cut through to avoid all that. I could, and just fight and get it over with, but nine times out of 10, they ain't fighting, they shooting. So to avoid all that, I just take a different route.

JAN: So does that make you feel safer when you see a police officer now?

TAE: Na, they ain't protecting me, either. They harassing me. One set of people trying to shoot at me and beat me up, the other set of people that's supposed to be doing good is harassing me every two seconds, so—it's crazy.

Almost overnight, Tae's social geography had been transformed. His route to work had been radically altered, and safe spaces he once frequented, like the Big Apple Games, the library, and many of the stores on 161st Street, are now off limits. Although the police maintain a ubiquitous presence in the neighborhood, they do not provide any comfort for Tae. Community violence and a detrimental police presence conspire to alter how he interacts with the neighborhood, in many ways confining him to what few innocuous spaces now remain. Tae is left to fend for himself.

Similarly, while Los managed to almost completely avoid police contact for the entirety of his young life, he directly attributes his recent arrest to his interaction with childhood friends in his grandmother's neighborhood: "I went across the street, down the hill, to say 'What's up' to my friends, gave them all a pound [handshake]. I started walking away—they thought they was giving me a bag of weed by the way I pounded them. That's when they pulled me around the corner. They stopped and frisked me." Seemingly benign encounters with peers in the neighborhood set in motion a series of events that caused Los to miss shifts at work, ultimately compromising his position with the company, as well as to miss class time during the college's winter session, during which the incident took place.

Still, others like Kareem, a 16-year-old African American high school student, remain optimistic about police work despite frequent negative contact in his area. He readily recalls an instance in which the police positively affected his life: "They saved my life. Something happened in my neighborhood, a shootout—and they was there."

Much like Tae, Kareem displays a similar aversion to restricting how he interacts with the community. After school and on weekends Kareem enjoys playing basketball with his friends on the nearby courts. But he is also aware of the negative attention that simply hanging out with his friends in public spaces may garner. The previous summer he and a group of friends were heading back home from another friend's house at around 11 p.m. when a police officer stopped the group to frisk them. After a few minutes, the officer let the boys go with nothing more than a warning. But during another encounter, Kareem says:

> They body-slammed one of my friends. . . . I was in the park and they was outside the park. The cops came because something happened around the area, but we was in the park. And they was running and, like, one of my friends was walking and they ran past him and they thought it was him, picked him up, slammed him on the floor, and put him in handcuffs, but he didn't do nothing. They didn't catch the person they was looking for. Once they got him, they took him to the station because he was talking back. He got out the same day.

Although the police incorrectly identified one of his peers and brought him into the station for speaking out, Kareem and his friends knew there was little they could do to remedy the situation without risking their own freedom. So they remained silent. He and many of the other "achievement-oriented" young adults I spoke to have learned to carefully monitor their own behavior, drawing on an intricate web of observations and lived experiences.

These young adults have developed their own hyperlocalized set of rules, which they use to govern their interactions within the community. For many, that means identifying those who are likely to compromise their own freedom or safety, and either avoiding them altogether or restricting contact with them. They also gauge their physical space to help determine where and when it is appropriate to hang out and spend time, with minimal risk of community violence and police contact.

"Can You Loosen Them?"

Josh is an 18-year-old Puerto Rican male who attends high school near Fordham Road in the Bronx. He is about 6'3", with a slender frame, long black hair typically brushed forward under a half-cocked winter hat, and a silver hoop in his bottom lip. While he has admittedly never been an A student, Josh has consistently received passing grades in all his classes. When he was younger, he was active in sports, playing organized baseball as well as basketball and handball with friends.

Josh used to spend time in local parks like the newly opened space near the old Yankee Stadium grounds. Like many of his peers in the neighborhood, he has increasingly chosen to withdraw himself from the community due to a combination of recent interactions with police and neighborhood violence.

"Now, it's getting a little out of hand," he told me. "There's been a lotta violence going on lately and a lotta cops passing through to make sure everything's O.K.—I don't want to get caught up in the mess, and stuff like that. I either stay home, or, if I plan to go outside, I go somewhere far, like in the city or Queens to hang out with my friends."

Despite his self-administered quarantine, Josh now finds himself entangled in the criminal justice system and on probation. A year ago, when he was 17, he engaged in a lunchroom fight with a high school classmate. The fight quickly escalated into a brawl, with multiple other parties joining in:

> I was the only person fighting him and I had other people jumping on to me and trying to hit me and stuff. Then the security guards took me out. They took me to the main office and stuff—they questioned me what happened and all that, then one of the policeman handcuffed me and they just sat me in the chair and all that. The handcuffs were really tight—I was like, "Can you loosen them?" It took him almost an hour to loosen my handcuffs.
>
> I told one of the deans—they actually listened to one of the deans instead of me. . . . I had to wait two hours in the school. I called my mom and she came in. They told my mom I have to go to the precinct to fill some papers out and stuff, do some fingerprint scans. I had to wait in a cell for two to three hours, just sitting there. They told me I had a felony, a possession of a weapon, a misdemeanor. I forgot the other one, third-degree assault, I think.

As sociologists like Victor Rios have demonstrated, schools and other community institutions at times serve as sites of routine criminalization of youth.[12] Additionally, in cities like New York, the policing of these young men's and women's lives at one point extended directly into their own homes through tactics like Operation Clean Halls, an extension of the Police Department's stop-and-frisk program.

According to his account of the events, Josh acted in self-defense, and, given what he told me about the incident, one can understand why he behaved as he did. Countless other young adults have been involved in similar situations, yet they did not share the same fate. Josh's pathway into the criminal justice system is often referred to as the "school-to-prison pipeline." In New York City schools, black and Latino students are disproportionately targeted for both suspensions and arrests. For instance, while black students made up approximately 28 percent of the student population in 2012, they accounted for almost 63 percent of school-related arrests.[13] In addition to the criminal charges that resulted from the incident, Josh must now attend night school in order to graduate. While his friends skate near the Whitestone Bridge, he must meet every two weeks with his probation officer on 161st Street, 30 minutes from where he lives.

Though he is just a teenager, he is subject to the same conditions as the other probationers. More important, he must now remain completely free from contact with police for the duration of his supervision, something that at first glance may seem like an easy task, but given *where* he lives, becomes increasingly challenging:

> The police, they'll be like, "What you doing?" or "What's in your pockets?" without giving you a chance. They just stand

you up and hold you down and stuff, without even questioning you and they just check you without—it's because they
tell me, "It's a bad area, I'm just making sure." I'm just saying,
you shouldn't be grabbing me. At least question me before
you do something, because they just do it out of nowhere.

If Josh successfully completes probation, the charges will
be dropped to a lower-level misdemeanor. Even so, he realizes that even that could have serious implications down the
road in terms of employment. This is important to him, as
it is for the countless number of young adults in the Bronx
and throughout the city who have been issued ACDs, or Ad-
journment in Contemplation of Dismissal. In this situation,
the judge may adjourn the case for six months to a year and
ultimately dismiss it altogether if the individual remains out
of trouble for the duration of that time.

Due to the all too familiar confluence of race, class, and
geography, the likelihood of Josh, along with young men like
Tae and Los, coming in contact with police would seem to
be exponentially higher. These sanctions are not an "out."
Rather, ACDs, probation, and even parole simply take on a
different meaning among young men and women of color in
the South Bronx.

2

Growing Up under Surveillance

It's like you can't . . . you can't be who . . . who . . .
let me see a good way to say it . . . you can't
be the people you see on TV and expect to be
somebody from the hood.

—Grams

On a chilly February afternoon I sat with Grams as he awaited a meeting with his probation officer, John Latedes. As Latedes met with other clients in the front room of the recently renovated Bronx NeON probation office on 161st Street near the Grand Concourse, Grams, an African American male in his early twenties, quietly texted friends on his cell phone a few tables away.

NeON, which stands for Neighborhood Opportunity Network, was a result of a massive overhaul of the New York City Department of Probation ushered in by Commissioner Vincent Schiraldi in conjunction with Mayor Bloomberg's Young Men's Initiative. Located in "high-need" areas across the five boroughs, the program was designed to bring together the Probation Department and community resources. Opening in August 2012, the physical space of the Bronx location is much different than one might expect from a standard probation office.

Although the outside is a drab blue, with caged windows, inside the walls looked recently painted, with a series of round tables near the entrance. A group of older black women operate the reception desk off to the left. Graffiti-like artwork decorates the wall along the main hallway, and a plasma TV screen sits on the far wall. The only noticeable security presence comes in the form of a heavyset Latina from an independent security company. On this day, she is wearing a long-sleeved white polo shirt and blue slacks, and holds tightly to a black metal-detector wand. Unlike the courthouse across the street, which is fully equipped with armed guards, metal detectors, and scanners, this space is largely devoid of these remnants of the carceral state.[1]

Grams's Story

In many ways, Grams's biography is the archetypal account of young adults involved with the criminal justice system. His story encompasses an intricate maze of blocked opportunities and illustrates how, over the years, so many institutions, most recently the 40th Precinct, have failed him and others like him. I choose to focus on the plight of these men and women because they are very much a part of the neighborhood ecology. Moreover, how police engage with these "at-risk" youth and sometimes predicate felons (those who have previously been convicted of a felony) can have huge implications on community safety.

Grams's nickname was given to him by a close friend in his early teens, an appropriate play on both his birth, or "government" name, and the weight used to measure drugs. He is currently on the front end of a five-year probation sentence for selling crack to an undercover officer in his neighborhood. Grams is small in stature, although his face looks far older than his 21 years. He has a slightly unkempt beard and a short afro. Apart from a tattoo of his mother's name on his neck, and another on his left hand, homage to his crew, the YGs, or Young Guns, he is largely unassuming and reserved both in appearance and his overall affect.

Grams, who has spent his entire life in the Patterson Houses, a public housing complex located in the Mott Haven section of the Bronx, began selling marijuana at the age of 12, and soon graduated to crack and heroin. In the 10th grade he dropped out of school to pursue the street full time. Grams elaborates on how his descent into the drug trade began:

> I used to see my father doing it all the time. I felt he was getting a lot of money. . . . I used to be behind him and act like I ain't seen him when he used to stash stuff. I'd run and sneak and take stuff out. . . . I started stealing off of his stuff. So I'm out there doing my thing, feel me? Everybody got they certain color tops at the time. . . . They got either bags or tops . . . we still do bottles in my hood. Yellow, red top, blue top. My father had blue and then they seen me with them.
>
> I was young when I first started so I was doing it, so I was selling them for $5! "Here, take $5 bags." So people would come up to my father and see the blue top and tell him like, "What, ten dollars!? It's five!" He like "who . . . who selling them to you for . . ." He started finding out about me [laughs].

After the third time he caught me, I got locked up. . . . He like, "Fuck it. I see I can't control you. You gonna do what you want." He started helping me, actually. He started giving it to me. "I'd rather you get it from me if anything." Then it just became like that.

Grams's foray into the drug trade was inspired, at least in part, by his father, who later went on to become his supplier. Despite the fact that his father identified as a Crip, by the age of 17 Grams had decided to run with the YGs. Initially Grams and his friends would imitate the mannerisms and handshakes they saw some of the older YGs in the neighborhood doing, until one of the "OGs" (an elder in the crew) adopted him into the group. This immediately sparked tension with others in the neighborhood, including his father:

My neighborhood was Crip. My father was Crip. So then with YG . . . we both . . . YG and Crip was left handed—when we throw it up, we throw it up with the left hand and then the Crips didn't really like that at the time. So it was tension. My father used to run down on me, feel me? . . . So it was basically like my father tried to tell me, "Yo, stop them from doing this. You got these niggas robbing people, they making the block hot. Y'all rob somebody over here. . . . I'm trying to hustle! Cops pull up on me and catch me hustling." I ain't really think nothing of it cuz I'm like, "Man . . . do whatever." We getting money in all ways.

In contrast to the deeply entrenched gang cultures in cities like Chicago and Los Angeles, New York City has shifted away from these hierarchical street organizations toward more loosely defined neighborhood "crews," or semiorganized groups of young adults that are often more transient in nature. The New York Police Department has adjusted its approach as well, implementing tactics such as "Operation Crew Cut," which focuses specifically on young people aged 13 to 21 who are involved with neighborhood crews. A year after its inception in the fall of 2012, the program boasted that "police and prosecutors have conducted 25 investigations throughout the five boroughs resulting in more than 400 crew members indicted for crimes including murder, robberies, assault, and weapons possession."[2]

With access to a crew, Grams expanded his entrepreneurial enterprise into robbing—both stickups and snatching gold chains, which they would later sell at pawnshops. Now even more deeply immersed in the underground economy, having a gun became increasingly necessary. With discussions about gun control reaching a fever pitch nationwide, widespread accessibility of guns still remains an issue in New York City. Countless young adults, Grams included, have walked me through the steps by which they have obtained guns with relative ease.

For many people, this ease is hard to imagine, considering the perceived effectiveness of stop and frisk in this capacity. Yet, as one analysis revealed, the citywide gun recovery rate between 2003 and 2013 was a fraction of a percent, or .016

percent. More specifically, about 600 stops were needed to confiscate each gun.[3] The gun yield was only slightly better in the southwest Bronx. In 2011, in one 40-block section of the 44th Precinct, approximately eight guns were recovered per 4,882 stops, or .12 percent.[4]

For Grams, having a gun translated to a form of protection and a sense of respect. Assault rifles, glorified during the height of the crack era of the late 1980s and early 1990s, have fallen out of favor, replaced by less conspicuous pieces. Still, as Grams reveals, "I was seventeen years old in the hood with a Mac-11 [machine gun]." This was his first gun, one he obtained during a robbery.

His eyes light up as he describes the piece. "It's like a brick . . . like this big [motions with both hands]. I got the handle right here and then the clip. So you can hold it by the clip. It's a Uzi. It's a little Uzi. A little machine gun." He later obtained a .38 revolver, a smaller pistol, after seeing someone in his neighborhood toss it in the bushes while running from the police.

Now, with two guns in his possession, he ended up selling the Mac-11 to his uncle for $1,500. According to Grams, "That's when it got back to my Mom. She thinking I'm the gun connect. Everybody run up to me, 'yo, I heard you selling guns! I heard you selling guns!' Shit fucked me up with my Mom and shit. It was crazy."

As Grams demonstrates, those who want a gun need not jump through many hoops. When trying to acquire a piece, residents involved in the criminal justice system almost never go through traditional channels to obtain one; all that is really needed is a friend or an associate with a clean record. Here, Shawn, a young adult from the 44th Precinct, described how some of his peers go about acquiring weapons:

> SHAWN: Nowadays, you get a brand new one [gun] for $200–300. In the box. Brand new. Never been used, with a whole box of bullets. . . . In PA [Pennsylvania], you can walk out the same day. That's what most people do, they go out to PA, they buy 4–5 guns, they'll come bring them back, they report them stolen, then they sell them in the street. It's ridiculous. It's like as long as you 18 or older, I think it's like 21, you go to PA and buy a gun. I have a friend that lives in PA . . . he has a whole garage with an arsenal, and he just likes to collect guns, that's what it is.
>
> JAN: How about—
>
> SHAWN: Used already? It would probably be like $100. A little .22, you'd probably get that for free. You probably sit there and smoke with the nigga, become friends, and he'd be like, 'Here, you could have it' [laughs]. If it has a body [a homicide], they'd rather pass it off, because if you get caught with that gun, you gotta take that body. It's crazy. The game is crazy.

Grams was never arrested for more severe offenses like gun possession or robbery. Instead, he accumulated a number of arrests for lesser drug offenses involving marijuana and crack cocaine. His most recent arrest, in December 2012, was the first to carry a felony.

Grams's longest stint in jail took place in 2009 when he spent a month on Rikers Island for a crack sale. This brief stretch only seemed to affirm his street ties in Patterson, however, as one of his associates from the neighborhood was only a few cells down. "Basically the house was his that I was in, so I was good. I'm like, 'Damn. God just was with me just now.' My Gunna got the crib, feel me? It was a half YB [Young Bosses] crib and YG crib."

When Grams was arrested in December, his father was included in a separate, large-scale federal case that brought down several others in a crack distribution network in the Mott Haven and Patterson Houses. Due to the severity of the charges, Grams does not expect him to be freed any time soon.

Only a few months shy of his 22nd birthday, Grams is unemployed and living with his mother. Apart from a solitary summer spent working in housing as part of New York City's Summer Youth Employment Program, he has no formal work experience, high school diploma, or a GED. He has a toddler-aged son with his girlfriend, who, according to him, is still "out there" partying, drinking, and, perhaps most important, is unemployed as well. He is not optimistic about his chances in life, but he does not hesitate to reflect on how he got to this point:

Since I was younger I always said it. It came out of my mouth a thousand times that I wanna be just like my father. I don't want a job. I wanna hustle. It came just like that, "I wanna hustle." My father making too much money. He supporting me, my family, everybody. Feel me? I wanted to be just like him. Growing up in the hood that I grew up in, if you want to be a fireman . . . who the hell are you? You was basically . . . especially to have my rep . . . we out here gangbanging, doing stuff and you're talking about you want to be a fireman or a cop or something!? It don't add up. . . . So . . . it's like damn, how do I start from nowhere?

Staying Straight

As much of the data suggest, a disproportionate number of those incarcerated come from neighborhoods that are home to only a small fraction of the city's population. In New York City, neighborhoods that are home to approximately 17 percent of the adult male population account for more than 50 percent of prison admissions each year.[5] Two zip codes in the South Bronx that are home to a number of my contacts, 10455 and 10456, fall among the top 10 in the city in number of prison releases.[6]

This can translate to astronomical costs to the community. The total annual cost of prison expenditures in the Bronx has been estimated at $310 million. In the Melrose neighborhood alone, costs are estimated at nearly $33.6 million.[7] Perhaps even more discouraging, data suggest that more than 22 percent of Bronx youth age 16–24 are considered "disconnected" as they are not working ("on the books") and are not enrolled in school. This rate is the highest in the city. In the Mott Haven and Melrose sections of the borough, this number spikes to nearly 36 percent.[8]

Grams is but one face among many trying to "get by" with a felony. As much of the prisoner reentry literature indicates, this is often an uphill battle fraught with restrictions on housing, employment, voting rights, and even educational opportunities.[9] For residents of the southwest Bronx, these barriers to reentry are compounded by a looming police presence that can hinder their ability to remain outside of the law.

* * *

Reese, who is 20, has recently reached the halfway point of his five-year probation sentence, part of a "6–5" split (six months in jail and five years on probation) the judge ordered for him after being arrested for robbery when he was 17. Although Reese received a felony as part of his conviction, his record is now sealed as part of the "Youthful Offender" adjudication.[10]

For Reese, "coming home" presented its own set of unique issues with his peers back home in the Webster Houses, a public housing complex in the 42nd Precinct. "I'm known by everybody over there and stuff like that," he said. "When I came home and just started acting different, everybody was looking at me, like . . . that's not the Reese we knew from before." Reese tried to go "straight" by minimizing the contact he had with his old crew in the neighborhood, often staying indoors for extended periods to avoid seeing his former peers.

He elaborates on his transformation: "[Before] I'd just ride out for my homeboys. So, whatever, if they was like 'Oh, we doing this,' I'm doing that too. So, that's how it was until reality hit me and I got arrested. Nobody was there but me. I ain't have no homeboys. I ain't have no family."

His incarceration and the feelings of abandonment that followed seemed to serve as a turning point. Both his real and kinship families had abandoned him while he was incarcerated. As a result, when he was released, he tried to focus inwards by obtaining "on the books" employment, most recently through a seasonal job at a nearby Party City store. Reese dropped out of school in the 10th grade and is now trying to go back and get his GED.

His efforts to stay on the straight and narrow are continuously stifled by police in his neighborhood. Over the past 12 months, Reese reports that he has been stopped and frisked more than 30 times. Additionally, the previous October, while spending time with friends, the police raided his apartment. According to Reese, a friend had recently bought a phone on the street, which, as it turned out, was stolen. Using the GPS system on the device, police followed the phone to Reese's place. Despite the friend admitting that the phone was his, officers handcuffed and arrested both youths as well as Reese's younger brother:

I'm like, "What is this for, Officer?" He was like, "Don't worry about it! Shut your effin' mouth!" Just talking crazy, so I'm like, "all right." We get down to the Precinct. Now, they put us all in a lineup. They ain't put my brother in a lineup because he don't really got a criminal background. Because me and my friend got the criminal background, they automatically, basically tried to railroad us.

So they put us in a lineup and the person ain't pick us out cuz it wasn't us that did anything. So they tried to make me

and my friend go against us, telling us that, well, he was telling on me saying that I did it. I told them, saying that he did
it, whatever the case may be . . . they sent us to the DA's office
because they couldn't get nothing from us, so they put us on
camera and stuff, and they was "blah blah blah blah blah."

And I was telling them that one of the officers told me to
tell them that I did it, or they was going to go to my house
and take my brothers away. They was going to send ACS
[Administration for Children's Services] to my house and
take my brothers away. So I'm like, "Alright, I did the crime."
I said it on camera to the DA that the officer told me to do it
or this was going to happen. So they seen it on camera and
they let me go from Rikers. I was already on Rikers being
processed, so I'm thinking to myself what did I do to be in
here, and stuff like that? And they just called and said I had
bail. I ain't really have bail, they just let me go, because they
ain't have no evidence on me.

Reese's already profound sense of vulnerability was further magnified by the series of events that followed the police raid—the coercive interrogation techniques and, perhaps
most notably, the threat of being separated from his brothers. Despite what transpired, Reese feels fortunate he was
not reincarcerated. His friend was not so lucky, however, and
ended up doing a year upstate for his role in the incident.
As is apparent in Reese's story, aggressive police tactics often
go beyond the street and extend into the homes of residents
in so-called high-risk neighborhoods. He feels that he was
unfairly targeted because of his past (although his record is

technically sealed). Reese is aware of his precarious situation and, in his view, tried to "do the right thing" by not hanging out with his old crew on the benches outside. As he recounts:

> They wanted me because my record is basically bad. They was basically trying to do everything in they power to get me arrested. That's why they sent me to Rikers. I came home the same day, and I'm just messed up in the head, like, what did I do? I just came home. I'm not trying to get into any trouble. I stay in the house all day. Right there, that caused me to not want to hang with my friends or nothing because I don't know what's going to happen when I hang out with them. Anything can happen.

Like some of the more achievement-oriented young adults, Reese resorted to an isolationist strategy after "coming home" from his first felony arrest. He quickly discovered that even this approach could present its own set of issues that might compromise his freedom.

Mecca, an African American male who lives a few blocks north of Reese, in the Butler Houses, shares a similar experience trying to "stay straight." At 22, he was arrested for gun possession, after stashing a friend's gun at his girlfriend's apartment. The police raided the apartment based on information from a confidential informant. Mecca was arrested and given a plea deal: "They started off trying to give me a felony, but it became some type of misdemeanor, you know they got Class A, B, all that . . . some type of misdemeanor. I figured once they said misdemeanor, I could still keep my license, my security license, and I could just move on from there."

As a doorman at a midtown nightclub, Mecca works late into the night, often not arriving home until 5 or 6 a.m. Less than a year after the first incident, police again came to raid his girlfriend's apartment, this time searching for a gun allegedly used in a shooting involving a police officer. Officers from the 42nd Precinct, along with those from an ATF (Bureau of Alcohol, Tobacco, Firearms, and Explosives) unit, descended upon his girlfriend's apartment at approximately 7 a.m. on a Friday morning.

Officers spent the morning searching the apartment as his family looked on. The questioning and search extended into the evening, but no gun was found. As Mecca says, "I'm telling them, listen, there's nothing here! I've been in the hood long enough to know, once you get a gun charge, that's it, it's a wrap. Now y'all gonna be on me. It's a wrap. I'm not going to do it again. It's over."

The investigation caused him to miss his evening shift and the accompanying "under-the-table" wages he receives after a night's work, a valuable source of income he uses to supplement his earnings from his minimum-wage security job in lower Manhattan:

> I hit 'em up and told them [his employer] I'm not going to be able to make it. He was like, "all right." Next Thursday I ain't get no phone call, next Wednesday I ain't get no phone call. It kept going for weeks and after that I was like, I guess I'm

fired. No notice, no nothing. They just let me go, so it was just like, all right, whatever. So, damn near the whole January, I picked up one check from Madison, and from there on it was just like, struggling . . . I've been struggling.

Mecca is expecting a child with his girlfriend, although their future together remains unclear. The loss of his night job created an even more unsteady financial situation for the couple. Furthermore, the police raids have created a wedge between Mecca and his girlfriend's family. "Her sister, she don't even like me no more," he said. "They went in there, they broke something of hers, so from there she started flipping. . . . Her mother brought it up too. 'Oh, we got you staying here and you got police coming!'"

Mecca's attempts to eke out a living and create a sense of stability for his family are only made more complicated by his past convictions. While he has largely moved past this phase of his life, he is well aware that past transgressions will likely continue to haunt him. At first glance, the police search caused only a momentary disruption in the lives of Mecca and his family. Upon closer examination, however, the residual effects become abundantly clear, as Mecca must pick up the pieces and again try to improve his situation.

Violent Interactions

In late 2012, a video featuring "Alvin," an East Harlem teenager, went viral.[11] The video detailed a particularly negative encounter with police, recorded on his iPod, in which the teenager was verbally and physically assaulted by officers executing a frisk. The reaction of many New Yorkers was outrage. For those who had experienced this type of contact firsthand, there was finally something to validate their own negative experiences with police.

Many of the young people I spent time with were able to recount aggressive and sometimes violent interactions with police that they had either experienced personally or had observed. Among young men involved with the justice system, these interactions took on a whole other meaning, with a dramatic increase in both frequency and severity. Of all of the local residents I spoke to, this subgroup often experienced some of the harshest treatment from police.

As one African-American young adult, Marcus, reported:

> They [police] don't care, because they know you don't, you can't say nothing. One time he ran up on me . . . he just moved up on me like, "Motherfucker, don't move or I'll break your face!" . . . the way they talk to you is crazy, man. They just, they don't even care.

Others, like Desmond, a multiracial African American and Puerto Rican male in his late twenties, have experienced more explicit forms of physical violence. Desmond, who grew up in the Lincoln Houses, a public housing complex in Harlem, but currently lives in the 40th Precinct, described a particularly harrowing experience from the previous summer when a large fight broke out in his neighborhood:

> I left out my building with slippers, swim shorts, and a tank top. I went around the corner to go to the "loosey" spot, and three detectives jumped out on me. I didn't see them coming. And instead of, like, "freeze," you know, "get on the wall" so they could pat me down, the first thing they did was take my head and smash it into the wall . . . turned around on me and punched me in the face and then told me "stay still" while he was choking me. I'm like, "What is this for!?" He was like, "We had rumors, y'all had guns over here." Officer, I got flip-flops on with swimming shorts and a tank top where you could see my waist. Where do you see a gun? Why did you have to punch me in my face?

The search did not find any guns, nor was Desmond issued a ticket. The following week, upon showing his probation officer his bruised face and arms, she urged him to file a formal grievance. Fearing reprisal, Desmond opted to not address what had happened with the police. Apathy and dejection are unfortunately commonly shared sentiments among many of the justice-involved young adults I spoke to. As Charles, an African American parolee who lives in the 42nd Precinct, summed up the situation: "I think the mentality is like, 'What am I to do about it?' It's been going on. I've seen this forever. What am I going to do about it that's going to make it different? Even after me too, right? You get the mind-set, like, this is the way it's supposed to be."

Ambivalence

In response to many of these often horrific acts of brutality, I came to expect that resentment toward police would be consistent among the group. I held to the simplistic notion that a universal antipolice sentiment would be shared by all of the young adults involved in the criminal justice system whom I met. To my surprise, I discovered a much more complicated relationship with the police.

Despite having actively sold crack and marijuana up until his recent indictment, Grams spoke fondly about a particular officer he got to know intimately during his time in the street. Grams described a specific encounter he had had with Officer Schultz as a child, one in which he was granted an all too rare second chance. Although this encounter was in many ways an anomaly, it marks a return to an increasingly rare form of community engagement that otherwise seems to have been lost and forgotten in the push for more aggressive tactics:

> It was a cop on my block named Officer Schulz. Nobody liked him, everybody used to be like, "Ah, Schultz is coming! Schultz is coming!" Out of everything bad that I did, feel me, out of all the bad shit I did, I was always a respectful child. So for some reason Schultz liked me out of everybody . . . so he actually told me one day . . . I was probably like 13 this time.

He came up to me while we all on the bench and everybody surprised. He come up to us, "Grams, how you doing?" I'm like, "I'm all right." [Shultz responds], "Bet you if I check that pocket, you got a lot of 5s in there." So now, I'm looking like, "huh?" He's like, "Yeah, I see you going back and forth from that building." So, I'm like, oh shit, I got the weed on me and all that. I'm scared now. I'm like, damn, he about to arrest me. But he's like, "You're lucky, I'm gonna let you go . . . I know what you're doing out here."

Many of the young people currently or formerly involved in street transgressions implicitly understood why the police targeted them. In their opinion, they were harassed only when they "deserved" it and were engaging in illegal activities. Moreover, they rationalized persistent police contact and frequent stops as part of keeping their communities, where their wives, girlfriends, mothers, and children also lived, safe.

One young person who held these beliefs was Justin, a Puerto Rican male in his early twenties who does construction work for his uncle in Queens. He works long days, often starting at 5 a.m. and working late into the afternoon. He spends much of his free time with his younger brothers at his mother's house in Queens, although he calls his father's place near Prospect Avenue in the 42nd Precinct home.

Life for Justin has changed dramatically in recent years. Apart from a fading "20" tattoo on his left hand, there are few visible reminders of his former circumstances. Starting in his early teens, he and his crew, the Rollin' 20s Crips, an East Coast iteration of the infamous Los Angeles-based gang, began their careers as stickup kids. According to Justin, "It was fast. At the time, I felt like it was easy, you know. I tried hustling [selling drugs]. . . . I didn't really like it. I guess it wasn't really for me."

Justin and his friends continued robbing and chain snatching until, at 17, he was arrested and convicted of felony robbery. Even after being sentenced to five years of probation supervision, he and his crew continued these activities. Only two years later Justin was arrested again, this time for robbing an off-duty officer in Washington Heights in upper Manhattan. Despite having fled from the scene, his codefendant, another Crip, cooperated with authorities and implicated Justin in order to reduce his own sentence. Sentenced to eight months on Rikers Island, a sentence reduced to encourage good behavior, Justin made it a point to leave the gang before his jail stay:

> It just didn't feel the same no more. I felt like I was betrayed by my right-hand man. I felt like I was betrayed by everybody. And I noticed, like, they really didn't care, so, I was like all right, and one day I left. I told them what they had to do to get me out the game. Basically jump me out.

During this window of time, Justin made a few visits to a tattoo removal center, though the process proved costly and time consuming. As he explains, "I didn't want to ask my parents for money or anything, so I just went in [to jail] with it. People already knew. They just asked me what it was, and I guess they was expecting me to lie. For me telling them the truth, I guess they respected it, you know."

Upon release, Justin tried to disentangle himself from everything that reminded him of his former life. The police, who he once held in a thoroughly negative light, took on a different meaning in his life:

> To be honest, [they] make me feel safer. If I was a criminal . . . still doing crime, of course I would say I don't trust them, they're a threat. But, since I changed my whole life around, I feel a lot safer with them being around.

Israel, a young adult who has spent nearly a quarter of his life behind bars, echoed many of these sentiments. One afternoon, while chatting with two other young men, Tony and Gordon, at a neighborhood center in the 42nd Precinct, he offered his outlook on policing in the neighborhood. Much to our surprise, Israel seemed to largely empathize with the officers, downplaying some of the negative effects that aggressive policing tactics were having on people in the neighborhood:

> I probably did more time in prison than anyone here. I got more than five years and I'm only 22 . . . and I got a positive outlook on police. . . . police officers, it's like every time I went to jail it's because I did a crime. But every other time I don't get stopped or none of that. . . . Police always gonna mess with you if you doing something wrong. I never get bothered by the police like that. It's because I'm never doing

nothing wrong. If you're doing something wrong standing on the corner at 12 o'clock at night, of course . . . just imagine you as a police officer—you riding around see dude on the corner.

Later on, Israel, Tony, and Gordon had a particularly telling exchange concerning their experiences with stop-and-frisk policies:

TONY: I think there should be a better way they can go about it. Not just to stop you and say, hey, I'm going to stop you because you got a hoodie on. If you wanted to be like, "Where you think you going around this time?" and ask questions before you actually start going into the frisk then . . .

ISRAEL: Where do you think you at? They'll pull a gun out and shoot the cop right in they face . . . people don't shoot cops now? Just imagine. We thinking like civilians. Think as you being a cop. You walk up on a person with a hoodie in the middle of the night. What, you just going to talk to him? [acts out]. "Get on the wall!" . . . Think of you as a cop. Think about it as you got kids and you that cop. You can't think like that. You thinking regular like you from the hood. You being someone from the hood you don't like someone doing that to you.

GORDON: But think about all the people they doing that to that's just walking to the store!

One of the young men who best exemplified this complex relationship with the police was Rick. Upon moving to the United States, Rick and his family settled in an apartment in Mitchel Houses, a public housing complex in the 40th Precinct. Having spent his early years in the Dominican Republic, Rick had frequently seen officers try to extort people—"dame lo mio" [loosely translated: "give it to me"], he recalls, was a common refrain among officers. Yet by his late teens he found himself on the other side of the law, selling drugs with a neighborhood crew in America.

In time, he abandoned this endeavor, securing a job working security at a bar while taking classes at a local community college. In a journal entry Rick wrote for a class and shared with me, he documented this shift in vantage point, capturing the precarious position he then occupied on the street:

Once I turned 17 I became a corner boy, and began to have a lot more encounters with police officers. Being corner boys brought a lot of attention to me and my friends because the police would know we were up to no good and causing damage in the neighborhood. Even though I knew that what I was doing wasn't good, I still felt safe that the police were around, and that my encounter was with them and not with other street guys who only wanted to harm us so that they could take over. So in reality with the cops there I knew I would still live to see another day. I know it was a weird theory but I would rather go to jail and have my mom visit me there then have her visit me at a cemetery. Guess this is the mentality of a lot of kids who grow up in the rough conditions of the projects.

"It Ain't Never Gonna Stop"

Many of the young adults involved in the criminal justice system whom I spent time with discussed a social distance they often felt from law enforcement officials but also, and increasingly, from other members of the community. They are keenly aware of how they are viewed by the police, school administrators, employers, and even their neighbors. Years of being turned away or failed by local institutions, or both, have conditioned them into accepting their liminal position in the community's social order. Facing seemingly insurmountable barriers, some have come to rely on alternative means to get ahead, fully aware of the additional loss in social status that could result.[12] As a young adult named Larry reflects:

> I think being poor is depressing in itself. Just to think about it, like, know what I mean? Light's going to get cut off, you ain't got no food. You starving, you got to feed your kids, like "what am I to do?" Like, I know if I do this, these are the outcomes of that. I know if I do that, those are the outcomes of that. Just thinking about everyday things and it being so hard, that's enough to depress anybody. . . . Trying to still do the right thing at the same time. That's a lot.

The lives of justice-involved young adults are marked by few, if any, second chances. The southwest Bronx, like other "high-need" areas around New York City, is a second-chance desert. Whereas their white and affluent contemporaries in other parts of the city are continually granted second chances, seemingly at every juncture of the criminal justice system, young adults in this community are often defined by their worst act. Tactics like stop and frisk often serve as an early entry point into the criminal justice system, with some residents establishing an arrest record before they even hit puberty.

One such youth is Cam, now 17, who can recall his first trip to the 44th Precinct for breaking a car window in the fourth grade: "We was young. They ain't put handcuffs on us even, they just grabbed us and threw us in the car."

Only a few years later, at the age of 14, he received his first felony conviction for an assault charge and spent a few weeks upstate at a juvenile detention center. He caught his most recent case at the age of 16, this time for assault and robbery, again a felony conviction.

In trying to understand the plight of Cam and other young men like Justin and Grams, it is important to broaden the way we look at punishment in America—in a sense, to shift, as sociologist David Garland notes, from viewing punishment as a mere instrument and regard it as more of a complex social institution and cultural agent.[13] It is hard to ignore the impact the various tentacles of the criminal justice system have had in shaping Cam's young life. Sometimes, it's easy to forget that he is still a child. Still, at present, current practices seem not to be effectively addressing the underlying causes of his actions.

Cam is currently on probation supervision and must report to his probation officer weekly. Any time he is outside of his home, whether he is spending time with friends, on his way to GED classes, or just picking up his younger brother, he reports that he is frequently stopped by police. In the summer, this happens at least once a day. Still, given this overwhelming criminal justice presence in his day-to-day life, these stops haven't prevented him from participating in a series of neighborhood conflicts with his section of Clay Avenue in the 44th Precinct. There is a sense of urgency in Cam's voice as he tries to explain why his block is currently at odds with crews that live less than 50 yards away:

> CAM: Since young niggas walking through your hood, they just, they say something smart, they go get they brother, they come back, they gonna handle it, because niggas ain't gonna . . .
> JAN: Why?
> CAM: Just 'cuz. 'Cuz of respect. Just because of the name.
> JAN: It sounds like you lost some friends, why keep going with it?
> CAM: That same reason why . . . because you lost friends. That beef ain't never gonna stop. It ain't never gonna stop . . . it's just gonna continue.

The New York Police Department persisted with an aggressive policing agenda in large part because the agency was convinced that it worked. The prevailing belief among city officials has been that aggressive policing tactics went hand in hand with the decline in crime. In an op-ed essay published in the *Washington Post* in August 2013, toward the end of his final term, Mayor Bloomberg continued to endorse the ability of "stop, question, and frisk" to save New Yorkers' lives:

> Our crime reductions have been steeper than any other big city's. For instance, if New York City had the murder rate of Washington, D.C., 761 more New Yorkers would have been killed last year. If our murder rate had mirrored the District's over the course of my time as mayor, 21,651 more people would have been killed.[14]

Yet, as the stories of Cam and Grams vividly illustrate, these policies hardly seem to detract young people involved in the criminal justice system from engaging in criminal behavior. Research by criminologists Richard Rosenfeld and Robert Fornango further supports these claims, as their work suggests that stop and frisk has had a much smaller, and short-lived, effect on crime than initially anticipated.[15] Instead, the excessive reliance on aggressive policing tactics seems to do nothing more than introduce more young people to the criminal justice system, thus contributing to a form of net-widening.

As the data suggest, stop-and-frisk tactics have produced limited results when it comes to actually getting guns off of the street. As a result, despite an overall downward trend in gun violence, guns still remain accessible to those who need or want them. Moreover, for young people like Reese who are trying to "go legit," these policies do little more than pull them back into the tangled web of the criminal justice system.

3

Parenting the Dispossessed

Y'all good for stopping him, but I'm the one
who's paying for his crime!
—Glenda

I'm impatiently pacing in front of a brick nursing home on a
tree-lined block on the Bronx's once-celebrated Grand Concourse thoroughfare. Today is the 44th Precinct's monthly
community council meeting. It is roughly 7:10 p.m. and there
is still no sign of Glenda. But within a few minutes, I see her
waving from the passenger seat of a tan Chevrolet Malibu.
The car parallel parks, and her friend Leslie climbs out of the
back seat. Glenda and her husband, Todd, whom I haven't
seen in more than a year, join us.

Todd is brown-skinned, with neatly cropped hair. His
shoulders are hunched and his eyes glassy. He is wearing
dusty blue jeans, Timberland boots, and a worn blue T-shirt
from his construction job.

He shakes my hand and begins to take out a cigarette before realizing that we're late. "Man, I just got out of work," he
says in his gravelly voice as he tucks it back in his pocket. "A
man needs a cigarette, you know?," he adds with a laugh. "Aw,
shit, we gotta go inside, huh?"

We make our way through the front door of the drab brick building and sign in at the front desk. Glenda and Leslie seem to take this seriously—writing out their names neatly. Glenda writes Todd's information for him as well.

Arriving on the second floor, we make our way to a large conference room that is almost fully packed. At the front of the room sits an elderly black woman wearing a Yankees cap. She is flanked by a middle-aged Latina and a skinny white male officer whose white button-down shirt is adorned with his badge and an array of medals and decorations.

On one side of the room a number of teenage Explorers, a New York Police Department–sponsored youth group, are busy readying materials for the meeting. There are approximately 15 rows of chairs, with 10 chairs in each row, all of them filled. After we grab some paperwork and sign in at the front, Glenda picks out a row near the back where the four of us sit.

The older woman opens the meeting, which starts with the Pledge of Allegiance and a moment of silence honoring the victims of the September 11 attacks. Leslie remains seated for the first part of the pledge, before Glenda yanks her by her arm. "Leslie, get up!," she whispers loudly.

The older woman, who seems to be running the session, introduces a terrorism specialist from the New York Police Department. He begins to expound on who terrorists are ("they can be anyone"), and identifies some Puerto Rican and black nationalist groups as terrorist organizations. Seemingly out of the blue, Todd stands up and makes his way down the aisle, muttering under his breath, "Y'all are the goddamn terrorists!" I initially assumed he was just heading to the bathroom, but then Glenda whispers to me, "He couldn't take it. He left for good."

Roughly 20 minutes later, Glenda and Leslie followed suit. They are tired. After working a full day, they do not wish to hear officers from the 44th Precinct boast about how crime has declined in the neighborhood. The more important questions have to do with why their sons are so often thrust into the middle of situations that can prove deeply troublesome and sometimes dangerous. They would rather hear solutions.

Although the three are long-time residents of the neighborhood, this was their first time attending a precinct community meeting. The decision to attend was not part of some grand plan to become more civic-minded. Rather, it was fueled largely by how their own sons, now in their late teens and early twenties, have systematically been mistreated by local police officers.

When I first met Glenda, a few years earlier, we sat on a cement segment of space near the entrance of her building in the courtyard of her apartment complex. It was hot out, and we were clinging to the shade. As we made small talk about the neighborhood, she proudly pointed to the perch on which we were sitting and then motioned to the ground, "This is my porch," she said with a smile. "And this," she added with a laugh, pointing to a space a few feet in front of her, "is my veranda."

Combined, Todd, Glenda, and Leslie have lived in their South Bronx neighborhood for nearly a century. It is their

FIGURE 3.1. A mother and her child attempt to beat the summer heat. Photo courtesy of the author.

home. Each has created family here, both through blood ties and kinship networks. Recently, however, the physical space, the apartments and houses where they lay their heads, and the public parks, stores, and streets where they spend much of their time, has been compromised by police efforts to make the community more "livable."

While so many of the residents I've spoken to in the course of my research recognize and appreciate the decrease in specific crimes, such as homicide, they are quick to acknowledge the profound social consequences taken at the expense of the community as a result of aggressive policing tactics like stop and frisk. In other words, while only a select few are actually committing crimes in the area, in many ways the community as a whole must endure the policing regime, experiencing a form of collective punishment. And nowhere has this phenomenon become more abundantly clear than among neighborhood parents.

In talking with the partners of men serving time in California's San Quentin Prison, the sociologist Megan Comfort concluded that the lives of these families are disrupted and consequently reshaped by the experience of incarceration.[1] They, in turn, experience a form of "secondary prisonization." Using this theoretical framework, I argue that although the parents in the southwest Bronx are often not the direct subjects of aggressive policing tactics, they experience an acute form of trauma vicariously through their children, a "secondary policing" of sorts, and must often endure both the emotional and financial burden of their children's interactions with the police.

A Crash Course in Parenting the Policed

For Glenda, the stresses of having a teenage son in the neighborhood have been lifted, at least in part. Although it is still only fall, this is the first time in years she can recall not being anxiety-ridden about the forthcoming spring and summer months. It is during these warmer months, when her oldest son, Richard, and his friends spend their time playing basketball or passing time on the front stoop, that they also experience a great deal of harassment from police. Richard is now working two jobs and has moved out of the house, and, perhaps more significantly, out of the neighborhood he has called home for the entirety of his young life.

Although Glenda has fond memories of times with her children in the neighborhood, more recently, given local violence and aggressive police tactics, the neighborhood has become a source of frustration and even anguish. Glenda is unhappy that she can no longer see her son as often as she would like. Still, she feels that his new apartment in the North Bronx, away from family and friends, is a safer haven for him at this point in his life:

> It was for the better, you know—him and his father wasn't getting along too well, you know . . . working down there, he don't have to worry about people coming in and messing with him. He don't know nobody that live down there, so it's good for him. When he comes back up here now, he's not involved with all that stuff going on in the courtyard. It's just "hi" and "bye." He comes over to see his momma and his brother and that's it.

According to Glenda, Richard's first interactions with police began in his early teens. She is quick to point out, however, that they may have actually begun long before that. "As far as I know," she says, "it could have been 14. It could have been younger, because like . . . the young men now, or the adolescents or young teenagers, and especially the men. I found out, that it became a thing with them, that it was normal. To them, it was normal. It was no need to tell Mom."

When Richard turned 14, Glenda had bought him the once highly popular Sidekick cellphone. One day, on the way back from school, the police stopped him and his friends.

During the search, his phone fell out of the pocket and broke. Only then did he tell his mother what had happened:

> He was on fire, he was like, "He [the officer] gonna break my phone and then start laughing!" I was like, who? He said the cops. I was like, what he stop you for? He was like, "Mom, c'mon!" He getting frustrated, like, "Mom, they always do that! That ain't the first time that they did that!" I was like, wait a minute, that ain't the first time? He was like, "Mom, this ain't the first time. They been doing that . . . I'm just mad about my phone!" I'm talking about, they been stopping you for what? So, I'm like, oh, wow. Then you feel bad because if something happens, you as a parent want to defend your kid. So, that's like a bully messing with my kid and it's nothing I could do about it because it's on a day-to-day basis.

Both Richard and his mother felt paralyzed by the interaction. While Richard was more immediately concerned about his cellphone, Glenda realized the significance of this series of events and how they might continue to affect her son and undermine her role as a parent. From this point forward, she said, she began to focus on how the police had begun to shape Richard's everyday movements.

This was her introduction to raising heavily policed children. Routine events like walking to and from the subway, the park, or the store became much more of a challenge for Richard and his friends. Upon seeing boys in groups larger than four, police would quickly break up the pack, splitting them off into pairs, and, in the case of an odd number, forcing them to travel on their own. Because her son was often the tallest in the group, Glenda believed that he was unfairly ostracized and pushed to go places by himself, using routes he might not have been familiar with, at the insistence of the officers. In Glenda's eyes, this type of police intervention could potentially jeopardize her son's safety and well-being.

"Thirsty Thursdays"

In the southwest Bronx, "positive" outcomes are too frequently defined by whether a person is able to leave. For Glenda, this came in the form of Richard moving out of the neighborhood. For Leslie, this came in the form of a change in her Section 8 housing voucher, a document that helps make housing more affordable for low-income families, allowing her and her son, Albert, to leave the neighborhood and move north to Westchester County. In recent years, as conflicts between local crews have escalated, the police have clamped down especially hard on the neighborhood. In the three years I spent talking to residents of the southwest Bronx, several large white New York Police Department observation towers sprouted up in the area for weeks at a time. Officers would also execute raids on particular blocks and buildings, using the program known as Operation Clean Halls as a means to enter privately owned buildings and implement a form of what is known as "vertical policing."

On the block where Leslie and Glenda lived, this resulted in a weekly event known locally as "Thirsty Thursdays." On Thursdays, particularly during the warmer months, police would descend on their block, typically in the mid- to late afternoon, and carry out "shakedowns" of the young men. As Todd described what happened, "They run up in here like an army, man. Coming up here with paddy wagons right up in the middle of here . . . you see they check to see if the gate is open and will drive right through the middle of here and start bothering people." A van would be parked nearby, and neighborhood boys were carted off to be booked on petty charges ranging from truancy to open-container violations or trespassing.

According to Leslie, these "scare" tactics are often used to badger people like her son Albert into giving them information about what goes on in the neighborhood. This can prove to be risky and even potentially dangerous for teenagers who may be labeled as informants or cooperators by their peers. For parents like Leslie, these tactics can prove both financially costly and physically taxing. During one of our conversations, Leslie and Glenda discussed the ramifications of a recent interaction with police:

> LESLIE: It's these stupid "disorderly conducts"—what does that even mean? That, or trespassing or loitering in they own building! A few weeks ago I was sitting on my fire escape. I do that sometimes, especially when it's hot out. And so I see Albert, my nephew, and George [another neighborhood teenager] just sitting there hanging out and talking to each other. Doing absolutely nothing. Next thing I know, the police walk up in there and are giving Albert a ticket for disorderly conduct. They said

there was a call that he was gambling and shooting dice! I'm telling you, they wasn't doing nothing! So now we have a $120 ticket! I'm just sick and tired of going to the courthouse. It's already been six or seven times this year. That's crazy! But of course I'm going to challenge it. It's not right.

GLENDA: You have to understand, it's hot out and a lot of people can't afford A/Cs like that so we go outside. Outside in the courtyard is where we go to escape the heat and so if the police don't like that, what are we supposed to do?

As Glenda emphasizes, this form of policing infringes upon local residents ability to find a place to stand. Given the dearth of neighborhood resources, young men in the neighborhood try to find solace in nearby public spaces, but are continually discouraged from doing so. In hot summer months, with electricity costs soaring, getting access to common spaces in and around their own buildings often proves even more challenging. Now that her son has gotten a costly ticket, Leslie must now shoulder the burden of either paying it off (and thereby acknowledging his guilt) or trying to contest the charges. The latter decision could prove extremely frustrating and time consuming and may result in other financial consequences in the form of a loss of wages.

On the block where Leslie and Glenda live, benign everyday activities often take on an entirely new meaning for residents. Glenda described an incident involving her youngest son, Cliff, which occurred a few years ago:

My youngest, Cliff, is 14 and was with his friend who was riding his bike on the sidewalk right around here. So the officer tells his friend that he can't do that and told him he's going to write him a ticket, so, you know, my boy just starts laughing. I mean, it's just silly the officer felt he had to do that. Next thing you know, they got my son in the back of a cop car. He had his cell phone on him, so he calls me and I hear him whispering, "Mommy, come get me." When I get there, they talking about they going to write him a ticket. I'm like, "For what? Laughing?" I'm not going anywhere. That's my son. Let him go. And the crazy thing is the boy he was with who was riding the bike in the first place didn't even get a ticket!

Through such repeated interactions, parents like Leslie, Glenda, and Todd have been conditioned to expect this type of treatment from police, although they shy away from accepting it as a norm.

Aggressive Policing and the Transition into Adulthood

It is raining outside as Glenda and I sit across from each other on a sectional couch in her living room. An open window allows for a light breeze on this humid June afternoon. Outside, we can hear trains whiz by on the Metro North track less than 50 yards from the building. "I'm saying no," Glenda says, pausing to let a train pass, "my son shouldn't have to feel like this is normal. I don't care where you live at. This is not normal."

Yet for so many parents this sort of police contact has become the norm. Similar to how many of their children have come to understand police in their lives, parents have adopted an implicit acceptance of their presence and even begun to equip their offspring with strategies on how to deal with unwelcome police encounters. In the wake of high-profile police killings, black families nationwide have increasingly begun having this form of conversation, sometimes referred to as "the talk."[2] For some, the experiences of their children represented their first introduction to this type of policing. For others, this understanding was carefully cultivated through years of personally experiencing aggressive police tactics or observing close family members experience it.

Lance, a young father from the area, explained to a friend, Joey, how these norms are passed down from one generation to another:

> LANCE: I got a daughter. Luckily I don't got a son. But what I think it does to little kids coming up—in they mind it becomes regular. Like when they get older, cops stopping them, they gonna remember when they was little they always seen that. It's not going to be out of the norm for them.
>
> JOEY: Yeah, like it gives you that assumption . . . that's why a lot of niggas think like that now. Like growing up, I used to see my older brother getting clapped up [handcuffed] for stuff like that . . . so it gave you that assumption that all cops were dickheads. As I got older I realized

that there were some good cops out there, but my first assumption growing up was that this cop stopping me is going to mess up my night.

Fathering the Dispossessed

Raheem is about 6'1, with light brown skin. He typically wears a knitted hat tipped to the side and perched on the top of his shoulder-length dreads. He is 27 years old and currently on probation supervision for an assault charge stemming from an incident on a subway a few years ago.

Raheem openly talks about the mostly minor transgressions from his youth, of which there are many. In his teens, he found himself selling small amounts of weed, crack, and angel dust to make extra money. At the age of 15 he was arrested for the first time and processed at "the Tombs," as the Manhattan Detention Complex is known. "Going through the system for the first time wasn't pretty, because I didn't know what to expect," he recalled. "You hear everybody telling them stories, like, back in the day, 'You know jail is rough!' So, I'm going in there like . . . it wasn't a good experience, I don't like it at all, because now I'm in the system, so now anything that pops up, I'm there."

Fortunately, none of Raheem's convictions resulted in anything worse than a misdemeanor, thus not adversely affecting his employment prospects. At the age of 21, he had his first child, a daughter, Serena, which he saw as a turning point in his young life. As Raheem reflects, "I had to fall back." He now has a job in construction, and is working to obtain his GED.

While for most of his teenage years he identified himself as a "hustler," his priority has shifted to being a decent father. He and his longtime girlfriend, Sharon, preside over a full house. Six children currently live with them, two from her previous relationship as well as the four children they share. Raheem's eldest daughter lives with her mother.

Despite his age, Raheem seems to understand the gravity of his situation. He is acutely aware of the financial responsibility, which can occasionally seem overwhelming, associated with a family of this size. Still, he insists, he abstains from selling marijuana to supplement his income, as he once did, due largely to his most recent arrest. He was initially sentenced to do a 6–5 split (six months in jail followed by five years' probation), but ended up with a 3–3 (three months in jail, followed by three years' probation). As Raheem describes the punishment, "Hard as hell! Hard as hell, man! That's the only bid I did. It wasn't nothing, but just, not seeing my kids every day, hearing they voice, just being out in the world, period. Freedom is everything."

Like many of the men involved with the criminal justice system who I spent time with during this project, Raheem is aware of how the police may perceive him and he adjusts his behavior accordingly. He reports having been frisked more than ten times a year from the age of 15 onward, with harassment peaking between the ages of 18 and 23. As Raheem notes, "That was a rougher time for me . . . but as I got older, I'd say it slowed down after I turned 25. I started noticing the pattern, like, hold on, I gotta change something because what I'm doing is not working."

For Raheem, seemingly ordinary day-to-day activities in public spaces can become cumbersome. He realizes how his own missteps have shaped his current situation and is unwilling to accept a similar fate for his children. While he has grown accustomed to police harassment, he is adamantly opposed to his children, particularly his daughters, experiencing the same thing, often going to great lengths to shield them from it.

He described a particularly harrowing interaction with the police that took place a few months earlier:

I'm walking with my daughters and my older cousin and they [the police] just hopped out. I got my kids and my groceries and they just threw me on the wall with my kids right there! So I'm like, what's going on, and he's like, "Oh, well, you just fit the description" or whatever. This happened right there near 167 and Jerome. So, I'm like, what's the description? You can't tell me the description, but I fit the description and I look like everybody else that's walking down the street!?

I was pissed off because you don't have no type of consideration. I'm sitting here holding my daughter's hand with groceries . . . and not just one child, I had three children with me, three daughters. And now my daughters are looking at me like, "Poppy, what's going on?" I'm like, don't worry about it. They ain't got nothing else better to do.

With his children watching, Raheem was made to feel embarrassed and vulnerable by the police. He worries that incidents like this will not only affect his children's impression of their father but also shape the way they perceive the justice system as a whole. Psychologists have identified this indirect punishment as a form of "vicarious victimization," whereby relatives may experience many of the same symptoms of anxiety and depression as the victims.[3] As Raheem puts it, "I don't want my children growing up thinking that's the way of life."

Although he followed a much different trajectory than Raheem, Rudy, a Puerto Rican father who lives in the neighborhood, shares many of the same challenges. At 36, he is a former Marine who currently works as a superintendent at a building in lower Manhattan. As part of his job, he was given a studio apartment in Union Square, but he chose to remain in the Bronx. While space certainly factored into his decision, he was also reluctant to leave the neighborhood he has called home since he was in the third grade.

Rudy is the father of an eight-year-old boy, Carlos. As Rudy's son gets older, his patience with the neighborhood has seemingly begun to wane. According to him, the area has changed a great deal over the past few years, making him less eager to raise children there. Several factors are responsible for this, namely community safety and a police presence he sees as ineffective.

Although he is careful not to romanticize the way things were, he insists that there was some semblance of order and decency in the past, something he feels no longer exists:

> It was more of a hierarchy, man. I'm not saying it was a good thing to do, but at least there was an order, you know what

I'm saying? Back then you didn't have these problems . . . personally, with me growing up, I'm not going to go to an OG or an older dude and fucking disrespect him, because I was gonna get slapped, you know what I'm saying? Because either he slaps me, or my older brother slaps me, or my uncle slaps me. I was gonna get slapped from somebody! [Laughs] I was gonna get slapped or cocotazo [hit hard on the head], kicking my ass, like get the fuck outta here. Now you don't have that. There's no chain of command no more. There's no hierarchy no more, it's just to each his own.

Having spent so much time in the neighborhood, Rudy is well aware of how his community operates. He prides himself on his ability to negotiate different local groups, although he understands how police may perceive this:

> RUDY: I've been frisked many times. I'm not the type of dude to be out there selling drugs, but at the same time, I know a lot of people. So, I could be talking to you today, and two minutes later I'm talking to some dude that sells crack or sells dust or something. The cops come and they're, you know what I'm saying, they're going to throw everybody against the wall and they're going to put you in certain categories, even though you're not in that category. You know, I probably make more money than you do. I probably have a job, and I got a family. Just because I'm talking to this guy, you treat me the same way. I don't think that's cool.

JAN: In the past year, how often do you think you've been frisked?

RUDY: Altogether, it has to have been more than 10 times. In that area there, since last February until now, in that area alone, it must have been like six times. And one time, I was just coming from my job. I mean, you could tell certain people from other people. I mean, I got tools on my belt, I got a bag, you know, dude, I'm coming from work. They want to know what's in my bag, so I oblige, you know. They take all my shit out, put it on top of the car. You know, my papers are flying everywhere, they don't give a fuck. They see I don't have anything and then they open up my Leatherman Tool and he says he can take me to jail for that, I'm like, "Dude, it's a tool. I'm a superintendent to a condominium in Manhattan. You know, I can have you call ten people right now, so you can verify that." And he still threatened he was going to take me to jail.

Incidents like this continue to negatively color Rudy's view of the neighborhood. Despite his age and visible work gear, police persisted in searching him. He is unwavering in his desire that his son not experience the same form of harassment, and feels strongly that his chances of not being stopped will be better in a different environment. Statistics support the salience of geography in New York City. In 2011, the year when documented stops reached its highest point, the 42nd Precinct, where Rudy lives, recorded 12,414 stops, or 15.6 percent of the population in the area.[4] Comparatively, the 13th

Precinct in lower Manhattan, which encompasses the Union Square neighborhood where Rudy is slated to move, reported 5,252 stops, or 5.6 percent of the population in the area.[5] Unlike some of his friends on the block, Rudy's financial situation is stable enough to be able to orchestrate a move out of the neighborhood. He has already asked his boss to alert him when a two-bedroom apartment becomes available in the Union Square building. Fed up, Rudy elaborates:

> Sometimes I just feel like cramming my whole family into that studio and just staying in Manhattan because I feel so much safer in Manhattan. The Bronx is shit, man. . . . [My son] he's eight years old now . . . and, you know, sometimes I just glance at him and I think to myself, Jesus, the shit that he's going to be exposed to is just insane. That's why I came up with the plan, he's not going to be in the Bronx. He's not going to grow up in the Bronx. By the time he hits 12 years old, he's not going to be here. There's no fucking way he's going to grow up and see this.

New Beginnings

Trevor, an African American man who works as a plumber, and his girlfriend, Kym, a Puerto Rican woman who works an office job in Manhattan, are relative newcomers to the neighborhood. Trevor originally hails from the Baychester Houses, a public housing complex in the North Bronx, but has more recently lived in upstate New York. Kym grew up in the Wakefield section of the borough. She originally settled in the southwest Bronx about three years ago in part because of more affordable rent but also because of its proximity to the college in upper Manhattan where she is a student. Trevor joined her last year, and they share a modest one-bedroom walk-up unit a few feet from a busy thoroughfare.

In recent months, a handful of shootings have occurred in the area and a robbery took place in a first-floor apartment in their building. They see a noticeable difference in how the neighborhood is policed compared to other neighborhoods they've lived in. This they attribute to a number of factors, including its proximity to the courthouse and Yankee Stadium. Now that the couple is expecting their first child, these factors have begun to weigh on their decision to remain in the neighborhood. As Trevor said:

> I feel like I'm ready to move. I just don't like the fact that . . . me, just knowing that all the time, I always get the second look, the second glance from cops. They want to do U-turns and stuff like that, you know? I want to move somewhere where I don't have to worry about police like this, the "stop and frisk." . . . I came home and lived in a decent neighborhood where it wasn't a lot of things happening so they didn't fly around like that. Like, over here, it brings back shades of growing up in the projects, the way they are. I just came here in January [back to the Bronx]. But, I'm looking to move. I don't want to stay here any longer.

Like many of the young adults I spoke to, Trevor has adopted something of an "isolationist" strategy as a way of adapting to his circumstances. After work, he leaves the apartment only when absolutely necessary, preferring to stay indoors, even in summer, away from any potential danger.

Kym echoes this sentiment: "I just feel like, we go to work, we come home, we close our door, we stay to ourselves, and there's no real sense of community or socializing. . . . It's like, go to work, come home, groceries, like, it's all basic day-to-day things you need to do. If you need to leave the house, you do, if you don't, go home. Just avoid trouble."

With a baby due in a few months—they are expecting a son—the couple has begun to discuss their immediate future:

> JAN: How do you feel about preparing him to deal with police?
> KYM: I'm so scared about that. I have no idea. I just feel like I'm going to read a lot of books and not let him go out until he's 18! [Laughs]
> TREVOR: I mean . . . depending on how we . . . I don't plan on living here, so, depending on where we're living, up until he has an interaction with them, I don't feel the need to tell him.

Although Trevor and Kym are lifelong Bronx residents, they feel that the neighborhood, and even the borough itself, presents too many potential land mines for children. While other neighborhoods may present similar obstacles, the pair feels that life on the whole may be more manageable away from the city. As Kym puts it:

I have my heart here in the Bronx, but as far as raising my child, I want my kid to go to a good school district and have a fighting chance. I don't want him to think that it's normal to drop out of high school or to be stopped and frisked. I don't want to worry about that . . . or at least worry about it less.

The Second Shift

In the 1989 book, *The Second Shift: Working Families and the Revolution at Home*, a seminal work on the division of labor in the home, Arlie Hochschild and Anne Machung talk at length about the so-called second shift, or the "job after the job," when parents must attend to housework and child care. In the southwest Bronx, this second shift often takes on an entirely different meaning for parents as police add another layer of complexity. Many of the parents I spoke to have cultivated a set of coping skills used both to deal with the emotional toll of having a son or daughter handcuffed and taken away and, on a more pragmatic level, to navigate the system when these instances occur.

When Glenda's son, Richard, was still living in her apartment, for instance, he was instructed to check in periodically, as most parents require of their children. In instances when he failed to check in or arrived late, however, instead of calling the parents of a friend, Glenda began to call the 44th Precinct to make sure he wasn't being held there. This decision came after repeated occasions when her son was brought in and often unable to call and notify his mother until a few hours after the initial police contact. As she explained, "You know . . . after a while you lose count. I can count the times I had to get him. I can't count the times I ain't know he was there. I'd say in a year . . . at least 20 in a year. At least . . . AT LEAST. To pick him . . . to see if he even in the station. I've walked, caught cabs, stood there."

During the summer, Leslie took it upon herself to restrict the movements of her son, Albert, to a set of previously defined places so as to avoid police contact. For days at a time, her teenage son was forbidden to leave his apartment's courtyard. "I mean he can go to the store for me during the day," she said. "But when it gets dark, uh-uh. He knows he has to be in the house. When he's at his girlfriend's place, I tell him to take a cab back. It's not worth it."

Even while on the apartment grounds, both mothers see it as important to keep on "parent patrol." With her eldest no longer in the house, Glenda's day-to-day routines have begun to shift. For starters, she no longer feels obliged to spend her after-work hours monitoring her children:

> I don't be out like that. I come on upstairs. Since my kids done got older and I don't have to . . . well, the oldest one has gotten older and moved away, I don't feel like I have to protect him and be there on parent patrol because that's what I be doing, parent patrol. My youngest one [Cliff], he don't hang in here, he's got his little friends and he's at their house. And to be honest, it's a color thing too, because my oldest one, it was black and black. He's [Cliff] black, and he's got Dominican and Puerto Rican friends so, they don't . . . it's when you get a group of this one right here, or group of that one.

Glenda feels that the obligation to monitor the behavior of her children has been lifted in part due to which children her youngest son associated with. In her worldview, race and ethnicity play a critical role in how young people of the neighborhood are policed, with black children in the neighborhood receiving a disproportionate amount of police contact, even when compared to Latinos in the area.

Given what they have experienced over the past decade, Leslie and Glenda are hopeful that their sons will "age out" of being police targets. These past few years have proved to be taxing for both mothers, as each arrest often takes a substantial amount of time out of their schedules, can be costly, and, perhaps most important, could compromise their children's ability to live normal, healthy teenage lives. Both Glenda and Leslie actively contested all of the charges levied against their sons. They take each contact with police seriously, worrying how it may negatively affect their sons in the future. In Leslie's case, after nearly two years of contesting a case involving her son and a friend, the matter was finally dismissed after a new assistant district attorney took on the case:

> We were out there, we came out to the courthouse the other week. The line was stretched all the way out here! [motions to 163rd Street and Morris Avenue, two blocks away from the courthouse.] So we waited and waited. We saw people we knew and let them cut, I mean we might as well wait together, right? [Laughs] So we waiting for some hours and I'm calling my lawyer, and she finally tells us that the case was going to be thrown out. They wanted them to cop to another

charge, but we wasn't doing that. You're not gonna have my son copping to something he didn't do. So we took it to trial and they finally threw it out! After all these years going back and forth to court.

In another incident, Glenda's son was arrested for trespassing while at a friend's apartment up the block. Richard spent the night in jail until he was able to see a judge:

GLENDA: They tried a lot of stuff, but, I guess they tried to scare him and make him . . . like, they caught him one time out there without me, for trespassing. He was 16, so—

JAN: So he pleaded by himself, you didn't even get to talk to him about it—

GLENDA: No, I wasn't even there. So you know, he was like, Mom—

JAN: Was it an ACD [Adjournment in Contemplation of Dismissal]?

GLENDA: No, I had to pay a fine *and* an ACD. He said, they told him, this how they got him . . . they said, "Could you pay $25?" You know, he want to come home, so he like $25, yeah! This is something he could do without me. $25. Then they say the surcharge is this, $145. Now it's too late [laughs]. Then, I'm like, OK, don't you ever do that again.

Tired and homesick after spending the night in a holding cell, Richard was eager to get back home and accepted the fine, unaware of the gravity of the charges. While he would have to see out the ACD for the remaining six months, his mother was forced to pay off the hefty ticket.

Glenda, who works at a child-care center, openly questions how things might have been different if she had worked elsewhere. Her office is in walking distance of both her apartment and the precinct. As a result, she can leave and check in with her children with relative ease and without a substantial loss of earnings. Had the situation been different, she wonders if she would have been able to put in the hours necessary to fight the charges levied against her son:

> I have a job that I can just run out and run back to. You really have to, because you don't know how long it's gonna take. So, yeah, you had to take off. You had to because then you don't know if your child . . . you telling me that he's old enough but he . . . if you tell him he can go home and there's an ACD, six months out of trouble, he ain't paying no fine. He gonna take that. But eventually, it's not gonna look good once some judge opens it up.

"I Know It's Gonna Change": Dislocation in the Southwest Bronx

For Glenda, the neighborhood has changed a great deal since she moved up from Maryland in the early 1980s. Initially settling with an aunt in the southwest Bronx, she ended up moving several times, each time within a few blocks of where she currently lives. She knows the area well, and from time to time she will reflect on just how much the neighborhood has changed over the years.

Although the Bronx of previous decades is vividly remembered as a powerful symbol of social disorder, defined by crime, drugs, and widespread civic indifference, many older residents remember these years as having a greater sense of cohesiveness and community. As part of this collective memory, mothers like Glenda often yearn for the "community policing" of old:

> The people who were in the area here, they were close-knit. Everybody knew everybody's kids. We knew people that lived in the courtyard that still live here now. Some of my cousins and them stayed across the street. It was just totally different. I seen it when, you know, police, at a point, you didn't mind. They were out there and it was like, that was their beat. They knew the officers that you was familiar with. Even if you didn't know his name, you knew that was the officer that was coming there. That's the police right there! The kids know the policemen and you had a conversation with him. When you was going to the store, you felt protected.

While some visible remnants of this form of policing remain, the statistics-driven CompStat revolution has pushed policing in the southwest Bronx further away from this standard. A direct result of this shift is families leaving the neighborhood. In my time in the community, countless residents told me about their aspirations, some distant and some already realized, to leave. For many, the tension between wanting to stay and having to leave was all too real.

Most mornings, before the sun makes its way over the horizon, Leslie will take a stroll around the neighborhood. A close friend, who also lives in the building, will join her on some days as they make their way through the maze of streetlights and stop signs. There's never any defined destination. Sometimes they'll stop for coffee, but usually they'll just walk and talk, enjoying the calm before the rest of the city wakes up. These are the moments Leslie misses the most.

In the spring of 2013, her Section 8 transfer went through, allowing her and Albert to move out of the neighborhood and to an apartment in Westchester County, to the north of the city. Although she sees the move as necessary, she misses the old neighborhood. They still visit as often as they can. She, to see her sister and friends, Albert, to see his newly born son, who lives with the mother of his child in the neighborhood. Still, Leslie tries to remains optimistic about the move and the changes it set in motion:

> LESLIE: It's really not bad. Albert is still up here all the
> time. His son is here and all of his friends, you know. . . .
> I just bought him a new bed and he hasn't slept in it yet!
> I'm going to return it if he doesn't spend the night here
> soon [laughs]. I spent good money on that! . . . It's real
> quiet there. I've been there for a few months now and I
> still haven't seen anyone who lives in our building!
> JAN: Do you wish you stayed at all?

LESLIE: [Shakes head] Uh-uh, not at all. It was too much going on. I had to get out.

As for Glenda, although she sees the rapidly changing composition of her block as somewhat of a natural progression, she is sad to see so many of her friends leave, and not by choice:

Well, I'm glad mine's [Richard] gone. I mean, whether it was the police or not, it was time to grow up and be on your own to become a man, because you a father now . . . you have to. But, to see families picking up, mothers picking up to take their kids, their young men out, because you're scared . . . both ways you're scared. It ain't like I'm scared of the street and I can call "Officer Joe" and he's gonna help you. Officer Joe is a big part of the problem. So, it bothers me . . . people that I've been with for years. Our kids grew up together. We still . . . it's a whole new . . . when I walk into the courtyard, it's all different faces.

With Richard out of the house, and her youngest seemingly able to avoid persistent contact with the police, Glenda holds tight to the notion that things will change again, and this time for the better. Along with a handful of her remaining friends, she has built a foundation in the neighborhood, and would prefer to see her commitment to the area through:

I'm not leaving. I mean, I work in the area, I walk to work. . . . I don't pay no carfare. My son was born up the block and raised here and went to school all around. The little one. Hopefully, it doesn't become the O.K. Corral, or the cops really get out of hand, or people just knocking your door down robbing you. I'm not gonna leave because I know it's gonna change. It's gonna change and it's gonna be a better place. I've been here for years, so I'm going to have to have this little apartment once it turns to condominiums. I'm going to be the little 1 percent! [laughs] I gotta have that 1 percent! You can't just kick me out! I'm that 1 percent and they better just build around me!

Still, for many of the people I spent time with, the damage has been done. Given the often-prohibitive costs of raising a child in New York City, aggressive police tactics pose yet another barrier for poor and working-class families trying to get ahead. This policing regime continues to undermine their roles as parents and has caused countless mothers and fathers to rethink what it means to raise children in the neighborhood.

4

Policing Immigrant Communities

Them over there, and we over here.

—Adriana

Having just ordered, Kwesi and I sat opposite each other in a nearly empty Benihana's Restaurant in Midtown Manhattan on a July afternoon. It's 4 p.m. and outside it is a humid 90 degrees. The air conditioner, which was blasting directly above our heads, provides a welcome breeze, helping to dry our already sweat-soaked shirts.

Weeks earlier, Kwesi and I had decided to meet for an early dinner to celebrate our July birthdays (his early in the month, mine toward the end). At Kwesi's insistence, we settled on Benihana's. He had discovered a few years ago through a friend from his church that if you sign up to be on the restaurant's e-mail list, you're entitled to a free $30 meal during your birth month. This is the third consecutive year Kwesi has taken advantage of this deal.

After we're finished, we exit onto West 56th Street, where a slew of cabs speed by us. As we make our way toward the subway, Kwesi tells me he wishes he still had an unlimited MetroCard so he could make more trips like this. It's nearing rush hour as we walk down Sixth Avenue. In the shadows of the skyscrapers towering above us, neatly suited men and women just getting out of work whisk by us.

Every few steps, Kwesi stops to look up at the buildings, awkwardly dodging oncoming foot traffic. Occasionally, he would break his silence by asking me questions about when particular buildings were built, or "who works there?" As we near the subway entrance, Kwesi slows his pace, seemingly taking a few extra minutes to soak in his surroundings. Then he smiles, explaining, "I'm not sure when I'll be back again."

Kwesi lives with his father and an older brother and sister in the 42nd Precinct, just six miles, or 25 minutes by subway, north of our dinner destination. But despite this proximity, this is only the second time he has left the Bronx in four months. Although he considers the borough home, unlike many of his American-born neighbors, his sentimental attachment to the community is much more limited. In many ways, the neighborhood is nothing more than a place to lay his head.

Kwesi moved to the United States from Ghana permanently when he was 15. He is a United States citizen because he was born in the United States, but shortly after his birth he was taken back to Ghana to live with his mother. Four years ago, with his brother and sister already having returned to the States, his father, a taxi driver in Manhattan, had sent for Kwesi. But although he was excited about seeing his siblings again, leaving his mother behind proved unsettling.

Kwesi has accepted the challenges involved with securing the proper paperwork needed to allow his mother to return to the United States, so the family can be reunited. "We always hope that it will be in the next year, but they never make it that simple," he says. "It costs money, it costs time . . . so that's going to be tough to put a concrete day on it. But we're always working on it, trying to get our options together . . . if not, keep trying to get more time and more money to do it."

Immigrant Bronx

Young people like Kwesi who have spent most of their childhood in another country, moving to the US later in life, are often regarded as part of what sociologists call the "1.5 generation." This so-called straddler group is unique from their parents, who have spent most of their lives in their country of origin, and the "second generation," who were born to immigrant parents and raised in the United States.

In this chapter, I will highlight the highly divergent experiences of six immigrant young adults. While they are by no means representative of *all* immigrant youth in the neighborhood, their stories provide valuable insight into how a cross-section of immigrants have come to understand police in their lives.

The stories of Kwesi, Saikou, Gauri, Adriana, Manny, and Ralphie take us to five countries spread across three continents. Some have spent a significant amount of time in their country of origin, while others have gotten only glimpses of their parents' birthplace through secondhand stories told at the dinner table.

While I shared common ground with many of the young people I spent time with during this project, it was with this group that I found myself reflecting most on personal experiences. As a second-generation American, whose parents came from India and the Netherlands, I empathize with the often-delicate task of maintaining a connection to the old country while trying to carve out a space of one's own in the new. Among immigrant youth, one can argue, the need for a sense of belonging and a place to stand may be even more important. Still, for some South Bronx residents with roots outside the United States, the process of becoming New Yorkers can be complicated by an aggressive police presence in the neighborhood, an experience not universally shared by immigrants in many other parts of the city.

While the borough on the whole, and the South Bronx in particular, is closely associated with its rich African American and Nuyorican history, as of 2011 the Bronx had a larger immigrant population than even Manhattan, with approximately 15.4 percent of the residents having come from another country[1]. The Concourse Village section of the South Bronx, home to a number of the people I spoke to, is one of the city's fastest growing immigrant communities, with approximately 41,748 foreign-born residents, or 40.8 percent of the neighborhood's total population. This represents an almost 18 percent increase from the year 2000.[2]

There is great diversity among these immigrant groups. Walking along 161st Street, I became used to hearing the usual blend of Spanish and English, but also, depending on exactly where I was, also French and Arabic, reflecting immigrants with roots in Africa and the Middle East. The people I spoke with and spent time with reflected the borough's rich

FIGURE 4.1. A neighborhood corner store. Photo courtesy of the author.

FIGURE 4.2. A group of men play dominoes on the sidewalk. Photo courtesy of the author.

diversity, with a great number coming from Latin American countries such as the Dominican Republic as well as West African nations such as Ghana. While other groups such as Bangladeshis and Indians are somewhat less visible, they are no less of a part of the neighborhood's ecology.

Still, as often happens, many of the young adults in the neighborhood have carved out their own unique geographies in the area, as I realized during the summer, when I spent a great deal of time playing basketball with young adults from the community at an indoor recreation program at a local middle school.

The program, which ran for a few hours each weekday evening, was free for local residents. And one of the first things that struck me was how the young adults policed the available courts. Based on experience, I had anticipated more of a division between Latino (Dominican and Puerto Rican) and African American ballplayers. Instead, what I observed was a division between some of the West African and American-born players. Many of the former were relegated to the tilted hoops furthest from the main entrance, and, when full-court games began, these players were forced off the courts altogether. I became curious as to how this division came about, and, perhaps more important, how, if at all, this might inform the relationship between West African immigrants such as Kwesi and the police.

The Protective Layer

Kwesi is 19 years old now, having spent the last two years of high school in the Bronx, ultimately getting accepted to a public university in the borough. Religion plays a substantial role in Kwesi's life, although it is also a source of frustration in his household. His father and siblings are Pentecostal, while Kwesi has chosen to attend a Catholic church. Because the rest of his family is part of a Pentecostal congregation, Kwesi often feels obliged to attend services with them, having to carve out time to attend Catholic services on his own. Between church, school, and the seemingly omnipresent challenge of finding viable part-time employment, Kwesi spends little time socializing in the neighborhood. As he explains:

> I've been going to school a lot on the weekends, so when I go to school, and then when I know that there's a Mass at a nearby parish, I might go there. Plus, on Sunday, I was going to study more—I go to school, I study, I do some readings . . . homework, I'm just reading and making small notes. After some time, I go to the church. I get it done, and then I go back and continue the studies. When the library closes, I come back home.

For Kwesi and other young 1.5- and second-generation New Yorkers, a lack of social capital in the neighborhood coupled with the strength of ethnic-group ties seems to provide a protective layer between them and police. Although Kwesi, a dark-skinned teenager, physically resembles many

of his peers in the neighborhood who experience a disproportionate amount of police attention, he has managed to
remain outside of the reaches of the police department and
has never been frisked. It is not that he spends so much time
with other Ghanaians, but rather that he doesn't frequently
socialize with many of his American-born neighbors. As a
result, he has in effect become "invisible" to the New York
Police Department.

The desire of Kwesi and others of West African background to not interact with other local residents has put a
strain on their relationship with some of their neighbors. In
turn, many native-born residents have begun to harbor negative feelings toward their immigrant neighbors, as, in their
worldview, *their* families are often the subjects of police harassment, while their foreign-born counterparts seemingly
navigate the area without any fear of persecution. As one African American mother revealed to me while talking on her
front stoop:

> They're out there almost every day. The Africans wilding out
> at night, and the cops will just watch them. Up near Clay [she
> points north toward a nearby park]. Most of them stay up
> near there. But the cops still feel the need to mess with us. I
> should have filmed them. . . . All of the bad stuff going on up
> the block, but they still feel the need to harass us here. See!
> [Points to a cop slowly driving by where we're sitting.]

Still, for others I spoke to, the so-called protective layer
took on a somewhat different form, as it did for Gauri, a Ban-

gladeshi woman in her early twenties. When she was eight, Gauri moved to the United States from Bangladesh after her father's name was selected as part of an immigration lottery. She explained how a simple twist of fate allowed her family to immigrate to the country:

> GAURI: So, one of my Dad's . . . he never wanted to come here, but his friend filled out a form for him, and then he got picked, so we ended up—
> JAN: Did the friend actually get picked too?
> GAURI: No. And the funny thing is, he did it in his name like three or four applications, and my Dad's name, it was only one. So it's pretty weird. It's always been said that my Dad's been really lucky.

Upon entering the States, the family initially came to Queens, settling in with relatives before moving to an apartment in the Bronx's 42nd Precinct. Although there were fewer Bangladeshis or Indians in the neighborhood, the apartment was affordable and provided a desirable amount of space.

Gauri does not spend much time in the neighborhood. She attended high school in the North Bronx, and, as a result, ended up spending a great deal of time in the area with friends who lived nearby. Her social circle began to reflect her school environment:

> It was mostly Jamaicans, yeah . . . and then a few Spanish girls, but mostly Jamaican girls from the school. I'm still really good friends with them. . . . I was the only Indian girl

in the school, so, if they said "the Indian Girl," they knew, everyone knew who they were talking about. Like, I had a few family friends through my parents, but that's about it . . . and I have like one best friend from elementary school, she's Desi (a person of South Asian descent), but she's like the only Desi friend I have.

While such a diverse social circle may have been the norm for Gauri outside of the house, within the home her parents held on to many of their traditions. Sociologists such as Alejandro Portes and Ruben G. Rumbaut refer to this phenomenon as "dissonant acculturation." [3] This typically occurs when a child learns the language and traditions of the host country at a faster rate than the immigrant parents. Gauri's mother, who comes from India and grew up Hindu, converted to Islam upon marrying her father. In their house, Bengali is still the language of choice. As Gauri reflects, "Even if I'd say something in English, my Mom would say: 'Speak Bengali! Talk what you learn!'"

The contrast between Gauri's home life and her behavior outside her home became more pronounced upon the arrival of her grandmother from Bangladesh. "I think when she's here," she says, "we're more, kind of Indian . . . we watch the Indian programs on TV and stuff, because she likes it and she misses home, so we'll watch it with her."

Gauri's parents still seek out "pockets of home" whenever possible, even making the long journey to Queens to shop at Indian grocery stores, which are almost nonexistent in their neighborhood. While Gauri's father has become somewhat indifferent to the neighborhood, her mother questions the safety of the community. Now in her early twenties, Gauri still feels consistent pressure from her parents to avoid certain areas, particularly at night. In Gauri's view, this is due largely to her gender as well as general feelings of unfamiliarity, and in turn mistrust, that her mother still harbors about other local residents:

> Say we need milk and there's a store right in our building, right downstairs, she won't let me go, she's like, let's go together. I'm like, it's right there! Nothing's gonna happen! She kind of . . . I don't know. She thinks, because I'm a girl . . . and, like, we don't really know other people so she categorizes them, like, oh, they try to stick together, they're gonna pick on us. That's kind of the way she thinks about things.

While Gauri has never been frisked herself, she can recall a handful of events that helped crystallize her understanding of how the police may perceive her, both as a woman and as a member of an ethnic minority. In one such incident, while in high school, Gauri and some friends were loudly passing through cars on a moving subway train. Two officers were waiting in one of the cars and immediately stopped the group. Gauri and two of her female friends were let go, but the men were brought to the police station and frisked:

> I think that was because I'm a girl, because it was me and two other girls. . . . we really didn't get into trouble, they just said don't do it again, it's not safe. It's dangerous. But that was it.

For the guys, and they were like, tall, black guys . . . they kind of got more attention for some reason.

Saikou and Downward Assimilation

Saikou, who is 23 years old, was born in the Bronx to Gambian parents. At the age of 11 he moved back to Gambia, living with relatives in Banjul, the country's capital. After seven years, he returned to the southwest Bronx to live with his parents and two younger siblings, while his older brother remained in Banjul. Before leaving America the first time, Saikou said he had several American friends. Upon his return, however, he says that nearly all his friends were Gambian. Similar to Kwesi, religion plays a significant role in Saikou's life:

> Well, I'll be honest with you, I do go to mosque every morning, but other than that, if I'm at work, I just make sure I bring my praying mat with me and I'll pray there. If I don't have the time for it, when I get home I'll pray. I stick to my religion. Five times a day, every day. I try not to miss it. Even if I miss it, I'll make sure the next day I'll pray it all.

As with Kwesi, the threat of being frisked is something of an afterthought for Saikou. He says he has not experienced any harassment by the police since he has returned to the United States. He spends much of his time working at a Dunkin' Donuts in Midtown Manhattan and hanging out with friends from the mosque. He aspires to go back to school one day to pursue a college degree, though he thinks that he may require a little more time to, as he puts it, "clear my head," before he resumes his studies. Saikou says that his father is extremely strict, and as a result he tries his best to steer clear of him in the home. In recent months his father has pushed him to get married, and has openly discussed the possibility of arranging a union for him. Saikou has been resistant. As he reports:

> They try to [arrange a marriage], but I told them I'm not doing that. Shit, I'll be honest with you. You probably could have done that to my older brother who's in Africa, but you can't do that to me because I'm trying to get my degree and everything else. I want to get everything out of the way first. Then after that, I'll think about that.

Earlier the previous year, at the urging of a friend, Saikou went upstate to cash some forged checks. The two were quickly arrested in a town near Poughkeepsie and charged with possession of a forged instrument. Saikou ended up spending a few weeks in an upstate jail and is currently on probation supervision in the Bronx. This was his first real interaction with police, one that he feels at least partly responsible for. While he feels lucky that the charges resulted in nothing more than a misdemeanor, he is wary of how his life could be affected by this transgression. For Saikou, this is as much a symbolic event as one with real-life implications.

Now forced to attend weekly meetings with his probation officer, he is becoming aware of how his interaction with police, and the criminal justice system as a whole, has seemingly expedited his process of "becoming American," and not necessarily for the better. In his opinion, "It's like the Africans are taking what the black people is doing, and the black Americans are taking what us Africans are doing. So, it's like, they're trading places."

Portes and Rumbaut refer to this phenomenon as a form of "downward assimilation." In their conception, while some young adults are more inclined to outperform their immigrant parents and ascend into middle-class comfort, others "seem poised for a path of blocked aspirations and downward mobility, reproducing the plight of today's impoverished domestic minorities."[4] As part of the larger process of "becoming American," some children of West African immigrants, like Saikou, experience an expedited form of downward assimilation through their contact with police.

As Saikou made clear, he feels as if his continuing involvement with the criminal justice system has him "trading places" with the African American men he sees on the street corners in his neighborhood and in the waiting room of the Probation Department offices. While up to this point he may have "outperformed" his closest proximal hosts,[5] African Americans, in some respects his arrest has seemingly undone any of this progress.

Mexican in Mott Haven

"I just don't like them," Adriana, a 23-year-old woman, says, her eyebrows beginning to furrow, "even though I don't have nothing on me or whatever, like, I walk through them and I just be like, speed-walking, or I get nervous. I automatically think they're going to stop me or say something."

Adriana becomes noticeably more animated when discussing the police. She is small in stature, with wavy black hair flowing well past her shoulders. Apart from a pronounced scar under her right eye, now covered by a layer of makeup, she looks much younger than her age.

Adriana is a second-generation Mexican American, born and raised in the Mott Haven section of the Bronx. After a number of school transfers (for academic and behavior issues) and some time off due to the birth of her son, she is, more recently, a high school graduate. Adriana currently lives in an apartment with her mother, son, and younger siblings in circumstances she considers less than desirable, explaining: "It's not good. Uh-uh. It's too crowded, it's too many problems. And then I don't work, so that's a problem with her [her mother]."

In addition to caring for her son, who is now eight, she is required, as part of her probation for an assault charge, to attend a "leadership academy" that focuses on anger management and coping skills. This, she sees as a stepping-stone to realizing her dream of going back to school to become a nurse.

Having spent her entire life in an enclave of the city with a rich African American and Puerto Rican history, Adriana has become acutely aware of her ethnicity. As she says, "Ever since I was in junior high school, I was about the only Mexican . . . in high school there was a couple, but not, like, a lot. I always tend to go towards where I see Mexicans. It makes me feel, I don't know, comfortable."

In Adriana's section of the borough, near Mott Haven, Mexicans are the second largest immigrant group (behind Dominicans), representing nearly 27 percent of the area's entire immigrant population.[6] Still, as a more recent immigrant population, there is often a great deal of mistrust between the groups.

A number of the non-Mexican young adults I spoke to used the word "Mexican" as a catchall term to describe all non–Puerto Rican or Dominican Latinos. In some circles, the word even took on negative connotations, becoming a pejorative term. For example, as one young person mockingly stated to his friends during a pickup basketball game, "that nigga look Mexican as fuck." Izzy, a Puerto Rican young adult from the area, tried to shed some light on just how strained relations had become on his block. One evening, he found himself having to stop a group of black and Puerto Rican young men in the neighborhood from jumping his Mexican neighbor:

> Where I live at, it's a bunch of Mexicans. You know, a lot of people like to pick on Mexicans and I don't have no problem with them, so I looked out the window and these young kids from the projects was actually beating up on the dude that actually live in my building . . . and he's a young dude. I'm like, why they doing that. And I actually went out and asked them, like, what happened? And he was like, yo, these people just want to pick on us. I was like, whatever, next time, I got you.
>
> So, next time it happened, I actually went out and I seen . . . he was scared to cross the street. I actually went

out and escorted him to the building because they was actually looking for him too. I walked with him to the building so he could at least be safe. . . . They seen me with him, they didn't even bother. . . . When I actually see him walking around on his own, it's like, okay, cool. They know he got peoples.

For Adriana, spending time with other Mexicans was a source of comfort, but also created a level of distance between her and other non-Mexican peers in the neighborhood. Due to the area's ever shifting composition, she at times feels alienated from the community, and has even become somewhat resistant to hanging out in public spaces she once frequented:

ADRIANA: There used to be a lot of Mexicans. When I was smaller, there was a lot of blacks and Puerto Ricans. There was a lot of Mexicans also, so they used to have a lot of beef. . . . It was fine for a minute, but then the Mexicans just left. It's only like a little bit. It's different now. Now I see different people. Like now, in my building, I don't know nobody. Yeah, before, I used to know like everybody. Now, I see people, and I'm like, oh, I don't know them.

JAN: Mexicans, and who were having conflicts—

ADRIANA: With the Bloods and Crips . . . actually, I don't know if it was Bloods and Crips but, from the Patterson [a public housing project in the area]—

JAN: What would happen?

ADRIANA: I mean they would just get into it. It was an everyday type thing. They would fight over the park, or just the neighborhood.

JAN: And so they would just jump Mexicans—

ADRIANA: It would be vice versa . . . sometimes they'll win, and sometimes the Mexicans. Yeah, I mean, but after a while they just kept it cool. Them over there, and we over here.

Until a year ago, Adriana's mostly negative feelings about the police were predominantly colored by the negative experiences of family and friends. As she said, "I don't like them, point blank. At all. With my family, it's been a lot, a lot of problems. A lot of violence with the police." Eighteen months earlier, a neighborhood fight that also included her sister escalated to the point where the police were called. Adriana was given a misdemeanor assault charge and a three-year probation term, while her sister, who was out on bail from a previous charge, received a two- to four-year prison sentence. "When she got arrested, I got arrested with her," Adriana explained. "It was like, we didn't touch the girl . . . the cops just took us. They pepper-sprayed us, they threw us on the floor . . . we was like, yo, we didn't touch her, but they didn't want to hear it!"

Much of my fieldwork reinforces the claim that young men are disproportionately the targets of police attention. In the case of Adriana and her sister, however, they were the siblings involved with the criminal justice system, while her younger teenage brothers had managed to remain largely outside the attention of the law. Still, Adriana remains worried about how her son will come to understand the police:

> He seen my family talk about police in a bad way . . . he seen me get arrested before. There are a lot of police in the neighborhood, so he just be like, "Mommy, Mommy, why the police is there? Why the police is there?," or "They gonna take you? They came for you?," or stuff like that. So, automatically he's like "I don't like them. I don't like them." . . .
>
> I mean sometimes, yeah, I used to talk to him bad about the cops, but then I'd just be like, oh, as long as you don't do nothing bad, you don't rob. If you do your thing and behave, they not going to tell you nothing. But he still be like, when we walking in the street: "Mom, Mom, why the cops is there? Why the cops is taking that person? Why they bad? They bad." And I just be like [shrugs]. Sometimes, I don't know what to tell him. I want to tell him bad stuff, but then I just don't tell him anything. I just be like, "No, don't worry, as long as you behave and you don't do anything, nothing's going to happen to you."

On Crime and Citizenship

Dominicans are among the largest immigrant groups in New York City. In the Bronx, they make up approximately a third of all new immigrants, with Jamaicans a distant second at 11.2 percent.[7] Compared to other immigrant groups, however, Dominicans often face greater levels of disadvantage. Many sociologists trace this to a combination of factors, including racial discrimination, lack of parental educational attainment, and language barriers.[8]

When he was six, Manny came to the United States, settling in with his mother and other relatives in the Gouverneur Morris Houses, a public housing project in the 42nd Precinct. According to Manny, after he moved to the States, it didn't take long for him to fall in with the "wrong" crowd. By his early teens, he had already been arrested for a number of minor offenses. These transgressions resulted in him doing stints in juvenile institutions such as Lincoln Hall in upstate New York and the now closed Spofford Juvenile Detention Center in the South Bronx.[9] Despite not being an American citizen (Manny has a green card), he insists that officials never raised the issue of his immigration status.

As Manny got older, he and his crew began selling increasingly large amounts of heroin in the nearby Soundview Houses:

Honestly, when you see me like this, I never smoked weed, I never did no drugs at all. I used to sell them, but never did it. Never . . . I mean coke, you know what I'm saying, I seen that before, but dope? I think that's the craziest drug ever, bro. Because that shit gets you sick. You NEED that shit in your system, bro. You need that in your system.

Spurred on by the profitability of selling the highly addictive narcotic, Manny and his crew, a mix of other Dominican, Puerto Rican, and African American young adults he grew

up with, became more organized as a direct response to police pressure in the neighborhood:

> They knew we was hustling and everything. It was always
> like . . . we had rules. You had a couple of shifts, from 9 to 11,
> it was like . . . it was like we had a job. A normal job. We had
> certain people from 9 a.m. to 12 in the afternoon. From 12 to
> 3 . . . and then from 3 to 9 . . . the last shift was from 3 to 9.
> At 9, we closed shop basically . . . no more, you know? That's
> how we had it.
>
> It was a dude on the corner . . . there's the building right
> here [motions to the cement]. He would send the customers
> to the building. There would be somebody in the building
> serving them, boom, boom, boom, boom.
>
> Hand to hand . . . it was always like someone on this cor-
> ner, someone on that corner. This is an avenue. This is
> another avenue. We had somebody on both corners to make
> sure the cops don't come through. They come through, "Yo,
> they coming!" Making sure they . . . once they pass by, mak-
> ing sure nothing's happening. But we also had them on the
> roof sometimes. We also had cops on the roofs, watching . . .
> yeah, it was crazy. . . . We just knew the whole thing. Before
> we start the shifts, we used to have somebody ride their bike
> around the whole hood making sure TNT [Tactical Narcotics
> Team] is not out.

In 2010, Manny was arrested on a robbery and assault
charge. Because of the severity of the allegations and his pre-

carious immigration status, the threat of being deported became increasingly possible:

> They were supposed to give me three years for this case. . . . They told me that if I plead guilty, do those three years, I'm getting automatically deported. So, the lawyer was like, you take probation, you finish it, you know you're going to be able to stay here . . . so I took the best offer, which was probation. So, I'm trying to do that. But at the end of the day, I'm trying to see, because I have a couple of people who told me about probation, that once you done, immigration can pick you up, you know what I'm saying? So I'm kind of thinking about it. Right now, I'm working on my immigration status . . . like, I'm working on being a citizen, but I don't know if I could because I already got a felony.

Although Manny has spent most of his young life in the United States, there is a clear risk that he could be forced to move back to the Dominican Republic, a country he has seen only once since he arrived in America more than 20 years ago. According to Manny, he has been able to avoid deportation largely due to his ability to avoid prison time upstate.

As he asserts, "They usually grab you up when you upstate, when you do more than a year or something like that." His codefendant in the case, another young man with Dominican citizenship, was also given five years' probation as part of his sentence. Since the initial sentencing, his friend has cycled in and out of jail for a slew of subsequent offenses, violating the conditions of his probation. According to Manny, at this point immigration officials intervened and deported him back to the Dominican Republic, where he remains.

In addition to the all-consuming fear that he may be deported, Manny must try to maintain steady work, an already challenging task compounded by his felony record:

> Right now I got this job. . . . I got like two months, three months probably, on the job and that's a problem, right there. They're telling me that's a problem because they took my fingerprints and everything, they looked at my record and they said that I have a felony and there's a possibility that they might not take me in the union. Yeah, so that might be an issue. That's a big problem for me.

Ralphie understands all too well what Manny's future may hold; after all, he was only in his teens when his father was indicted under the RICO (Racketeer Influenced and Corrupt Organizations) Act, a law typically reserved for people involved in organized crime. After serving nearly seven years of his lengthy sentence, he was ultimately deported back to the Dominican Republic. Ralphie, who was raised primarily by his mother and a host of aunts, cultivated his own unique sense of being in the world, in many ways a direct response to the way his father operated:

> My father was a hustler. . . . I learned crime doesn't pay, no matter how much cars you got, how much women you got. At the end of the day, what are you doing now, the next 20

years of your life. . . . How quick is your money? Do you have enough money to get a lawyer when the hammer . . . you know, when it comes down to it? That's not forever. It's rare. I don't even know how to explain it. You have a better chance of walking on water then actually being rich and getting away with it, know what I mean?

Having spent much of his childhood in the Soundview section of the Bronx, Ralphie's awareness of inequality began at an early age. Even before his father was sent away, one particular event seemed to sharpen his understanding of the role the criminal justice system played in his community. In 1999, an unarmed Guinean immigrant named Amadou Diallo was fatally shot 41 times by four New York Police Department officers on the doorstep of his apartment.[10] All four officers were ultimately acquitted. For Ralphie, these events in his own neighborhood made a lasting impression:

I remember as a kid going to the block and seeing the bullet holes in the door and not knowing what just happened . . . knowing that somebody got shot, but not knowing who it was and not knowing how big it was. That's like two, three blocks from where I'm from. My babysitter took me there. It gave me a bad feeling. I was a happy kid, I loved watching cartoons, wrestling, so everything was happy. I never was sad. I love my mother for giving me the childhood that I had. So the fact that I had to see bullet holes in a wall gave me this bad feeling I didn't like.

Like many of his peers in the neighborhood, Ralphie has developed a deep mistrust of police. This was primarily due to how he felt police often misunderstood him. In Ralphie's opinion, due to the combination of his ethnicity, the area's negative reputation, and the way he dressed, police would often single him out. As he summed it up, "Growing up in the hood and being the kid that sags his pants, you're already stereotyped as being on that side of the line, you know what I mean?"

In his view, police often use these cues in deciding who to stop. For Ralphie, one of the few things in his control is the way he dresses. Like other young adults I spent time with, he believes that a police officer's perception about a local resident is heavily influenced by what the person is wearing. Still, consistent with many of his peers, Ralphie does not feel that he should have to monitor his style of dress in order to conform to a police officer's standards:

The image I give off is how I dress. Not only how I dress, how I look. With short hair, long hair, I look . . . I don't know how to explain it. I guess, a lot of people who look like me, a lot of Latinos, Hispanics, young age, that look like me, already give off a bad name for me, so I'm stereotyped basically. And I don't help myself either, because I'm walking around with my pants sometimes hanging halfway down my behind and dressing how they dress, not necessarily, but, you know, the same way. Jean jackets on, you know, because everybody wears jean jackets. So, I'm pretty sure if I was to walk around with shoes and change it up with a collared shirt, it wouldn't be such a big problem. But I guess it's just the image.

In high school, Ralphie's sense of ethnic identity was reshaped. Having attended a high school in the North Bronx where most of the students were West Indian, he found himself gravitating to other Latinos, regardless of their specific ethnicity. Unlike Adriana, Ralphie cultivated a form of pan-ethnic Latino identity and adapted accordingly:

> It was very, very, very bad. The school was uptown, full of West Indians, Jamaican dudes. School was very bad. I heard stories about a kid using the urinal got stabbed in the back of the head, so my whole freshman year I didn't use the bathroom. Just a way to maneuver . . . people say it's being dumb or being scared, I call it being intelligent.

When dealing with the criminal justice system, Ralphie employs the same awareness he used to navigate his neighborhood and his school. As time passes, however, his perception of the police has begun to change. Part of this he attributes to age—he turns 21 in a few months. The other part he attributes to his schooling. After high school, Ralphie moved to a small town in upstate New York to attend community college there. He began taking criminal justice courses, and eventually decided to major in the field.

After losing his job in retail, and no longer able to pay rent and tuition, he moved back down to the Bronx, transferring to a community college in Manhattan. Although he was only gone from the city for a few years, his outlook on policing in New York has shifted dramatically. He shies away from canonizing the police, but at the same time he has developed a sense of empathy for officers, even going so far as to express interest in one day joining the force. As he says:

> Just respect them. Show them respect. If you show them respect, they're going to show you respect back. A lot of people give them attitude . . . "I gotta go to work, I'm late! You want to stop me for no reason!" I see it all the time. . . . One of my favorite shows is *Boston's Finest*. It shows a bunch of undercover minority policemen doing their work . . . and I love that show, because it shows undercover minority policemen! These guys look like they could be gangbangers, but you see them put on they vests and it says "Gang Squad." I love that. I want to be that.

Besides, he adds, "I'm not gonna lie. You on a train at nighttime and as much as you hate cops, you see a cop at the train station on the platform. You feel safe because you know nobody's gonna do nothing to you!"

Given what his father has been through, I was admittedly surprised by Ralphie's current interest in becoming a police officer. The transformation of his outlook seems to be rooted in his desire to defy many of the stereotypes that others, particularly the police, have bestowed upon him.

Moreover, on a purely pragmatic level, one of the more underacknowledged realities is that many of the civil service jobs available in the city's Police Department, Fire Department, and even the Department of Corrections remain some of the few viable career options available to New Yorkers that provide a living wage, extended benefits, and do not have substantial postsecondary educational requirements. This helps explain why some recent immigrants seek to join the New York Police Department, despite having grown up in heavily policed neighborhoods and experiencing negative interactions with the police firsthand.

As this chapter demonstrates, the police can play a variety of roles in the lives of immigrant young adults. For some, contact with the police seemed to expedite the process of assimilation, albeit in a downward trajectory. Others were afforded a protective buffer because of their ethnicity or how they interacted with the neighborhood. Saikou, for one, demonstrated how easy it is for black immigrants to forfeit their "protective layer," while Gauri, as a South Asian woman, seemed to be given second chances from the police precisely because of her gender and ethnicity.

For immigrants coming of age in the South Bronx and other "high-need" areas of the city, the process of learning how to deal with an aggressive police presence adds a unique layer to the process of becoming a New Yorker, one that immigrants in different parts of the city may not experience in quite the same manner.

5

Losing Your Right to the City

Why would I want to help you solve a crime or
tell you anything . . . and you talking to me like
I'm a piece of trash at the bottom of your shoe?
—Robert

Aggressive policing has affected residents of the southwest Bronx in myriad and punishing ways. In many cases, even momentary interactions with the police have triggered a series of events that can profoundly alter the course of one's life.

For residents like Reese, a formerly incarcerated young adult, aggressive policing tactics acted as a means of keeping him engaged with the criminal justice system, despite his attempts to "go legit." While others, like Kwesi, a Ghanaian immigrant, have managed to steer clear of police in their neighborhood using their immigrant "protective layer," this behavior has come at a pronounced social cost. Fathers like Raheem openly discussed the humiliation of being stopped and frisked while going to the store with young children in tow, while mothers like Leslie have reluctantly made the increasingly common decision to move out of the neighborhood altogether.

Young adults in this part of the Bronx have grown up on blocks where the sight of a neighbor, friend, or family member being harassed by the police is a common occurrence. As children, they are often painfully aware that their turn awaits.

Herein lies one of the more profound unanticipated consequences of the city's stop-and-frisk policies. The practice has effectively worked to reshape many New Yorkers' sense of citizenship and belonging in the city, particularly for young adults. It is yet another reminder of just how the combination of race, class, and geography can conspire to further solidify social caste in America, reaffirming how the state perceives particular groups.

As a result of these policies, young black and Latino residents are losing their rights to the city. In the southwest Bronx, even the quintessentially New York act of sitting on one's own stoop has become risky. Public spaces that were once relied on to allow people to socialize and create meaningful associations are no longer available. As a means of coping with an overzealous police force, my findings reveal just how common it is for residents to withdraw from the greater community. This, in turn, can have severe consequences on the individual and neighborhood. Aggressive policing continually discourages the creation of neighborhood-level social ties, the very ties that may aid in getting a job or further educational opportunities.

On a neighborhood level, these weakened social networks can have an adverse effect on a community's ability to police itself. According to the criminologists Clifford Shaw and Henry D. McKay, social disorganization refers to the inability of a community to collectively identify and solve the problems of its residents.[1] In addition to variables like residential mobility and poverty, "weak social networks decrease a neighborhood's capacity to control the behavior of people in public, and hence increase the likelihood of crime."[2]

The criminologist Todd Clear uses the term "destabilizing neighborhoods" to describe the impact that mass incarceration has had on communities. [3] To a similar degree, aggressive policing in the southwest Bronx has destabilized the neighborhood. When the young people of the community are continually forced to withdraw from its streets and public places due to fear of negative encounters with the police, the informal mechanisms of social control are weakened, ultimately affecting the community's ability to collectively solve problems.[4]

Resilience

On a more micro level, most of the residents I encountered exhibited a great deal of resilience. Violence from the police as well as their peers is a part of the social world of many young people, especially those who live in poor communities, but they are reluctant to let this violence define them. In the wake of aggressive policing, some of the older members of the community found solace in organizing other residents and becoming more engaged in local politics and campaigns against stop-and-frisk tactics.

By contrast, many of the young adults I spent time with directed their energy inwards. They already experience high levels of anxiety in settings like school and in the home, as well as among their peers. Negative interactions with the police add yet another source of stress, one that is not universally experienced by their peers in other parts of the city.

Resilience for these younger residents is demonstrated by their remarkable ability to compartmentalize troubling and even dangerous incidents and events in a way that prevents them from "contaminating" other aspects of their social, educational, and work lives. Among those young people who had the most frequent interactions with the police, the topic would come up only rarely. Conversations typically centered on the more mundane details of their everyday lives, with the police seemingly mentioned only as an afterthought.

I was initially surprised by this considering the frequency of many young adults' involvement with the New York Police Department. Over time, I came to realize that this was part of the compartmentalization process, a tactic that deflected the immediacy of the issue. For so many of the young adults I spoke to, to actually think about and process what happened in their encounters with the police can become overwhelming. As one young adult, Larry, had said, "Just thinking about everyday things and it being so hard, that's enough to depress anybody."

Ripple Effects

With other jurisdictions around the country already beginning to adopt elements of the New York Police Department's approach, it is worthwhile to revisit the overall efficacy of the regime. For a number of sociologists and criminologists, a central question remains: Can the continuing decline in crime be attributed directly to policing tactics like stop and frisk? Additionally, what are some of the unanticipated consequences of this approach to policing?

Beginning in the early 1990s, New York City experienced a substantial drop in crime. This decline actually predates the first William Bratton administration (between 1994 and 1996) that is widely credited with being responsible for the decrease in crime. Data suggest that crime was already on the decline before this first term and continued to decrease even after the New York Police Department began to ease its reliance on "stop, question, and frisk" as a tactic.

Moreover, a growing body of research suggests that aggressive policing is simply not a sustainable policy because the social costs of this form of social control outweigh its potential benefits. Findings from the legal scholar Tom Tyler and his colleagues show a powerful connection between police legitimacy and compliance with the law.[5] More specifically, they write, "when authorities are viewed as legitimate, they are better able to motivate people to comply with the law."[6] Moreover, research from Stephanie Wiley and Finn-Aage Esbensen suggests that being stopped or arrested may actually contribute to further delinquency, rather than reduce it.[7]

As is demonstrated by a 2013 report from the Vera Institute of Justice, a national criminal justice think tank, aggressive policing can have a profound impact on the willingness of local residents to cooperate with authorities:

Young people who have been stopped more often in the past are less willing to report crimes, even when they themselves are the victims. Each additional stop in the span of a year is associated with an 8% drop in the person's likelihood of reporting a violent crime he or she might experience in the future.[8]

This reluctance to engage with police can extend into the courtroom as well, negatively affecting a district attorney's ability to secure a conviction. "Thompson," a high-ranking attorney at the Bronx District Attorney's office, has been with the department for approximately 20 years. He arrived to the borough fresh out of law school in the mid-1990s, at the peak of the War on Drugs. With his docket in the 100s, he reports having felt overwhelmed by the sheer volume of his caseload, as he and his colleagues were forced to triage as a way to keep up with the demand. By the time the 2000s rolled around, things began to turn around:

> [In] '96-'97 . . . it was crazy busy. A lot of violence, shootings, robberies, assaults, guns, everything. I got promoted to a trial bureau like this one in mid-'97. My caseload then was very, very high. A lot of felonies. A lot of violence. As the 2000s came in, crime dropped. My caseload dropped. I felt it drop. I went from when I first started in trial bureau, from like 60 indictments, which is a lot. They're serious crimes, there's a lot of work that goes into them, to 30–35 indictments . . . and I'm not saying crime dropped by half, I don't know. I'm just saying, we all felt it.

With caseloads beginning to subside, community relations continued to falter, due in large part to widespread mistrust of the NYPD across the borough. As Thompson illustrates, this can have tangible effects on the conviction rate:

The "stop and frisk" part . . . that might be what effects the conviction rate. And I don't mean that by itself, but, like the Diallo case, Abner Louima in a different county. All these things that build up, because we read about it . . . if I read about it and it's on the news, the jurors read about it. If I read the *Post*, they read the *Post*. . . . Listen, a lot of jurors don't trust the police. I don't even know if they trust me. I think they trust me, but I'm not so sure. There's a lot of police officers—great, great police officers who are good guys trying to do the right thing and they get in front of the jury and the jurors are like "We don't like him." Because he's a cop.

Here, one can see the divide between community members and local law enforcement on full display. This pervasive sense of mistrust also extended to the process of obtaining witness testimony, perhaps an attorney's biggest asset when building a case:

So 18 years ago, I'm in that building, I have 80 cases, and I have my first, like, case that's in the press. It's a misdemeanor, but it's in the press, whatever, it was an MTA driver that got assaulted and we had a witness who was on the subway.

I go out to her house, her apartment, it was a freezing, freezing day, like a foot of snow on the ground. I go with the detective. It was my first time ever at somebody's house and I'm all, my eyes are wide open.

We walk into the projects, go up like five flights and we knock on the door and a woman says, "Who is it?"

We say it's the DA's office and a police officer. I show my ID through the peephole, she says hold on a second, hold on. She comes and opens a door, it's an older woman. I say, hi, we're looking for so and so, I think it's your daughter. She goes, she's not here. I said, it's freezing . . . can we come in? She says sure.

We go into her kitchen, it's freezing, and she said, what are you doing? So I said, she's a witness to a crime, she's not in trouble, but I really would like to speak to her. She said, are you sure she's not in trouble? I said, ma'am, I'm telling you, she's a witness, she saw a guy get assaulted, we'd really like to speak to her. She goes, hold on a second. She goes to the fire escape, opens the window and tells her daughter to come back in. Her daughter was on the fire escape. It had to be 10 degrees out. She was hiding. She comes in. She makes tea for us. The girl was 16. We sit down, we have tea. She's the nicest girl in the world . . . distrusted anybody in a uniform. Anybody.

Repeat negative interactions with street-level bureaucrats[9] like the New York Police Department not only produce damaging effects on a community level, but can also impact how justice is dispensed. In Thompson's conception, due in part to aggressive police tactics, jurors and witnesses alike seemed less likely to sympathize with police officers, thus at times affecting his ability to secure a conviction.

Policy Implications

Two white vans with blue trim speed by Robert and me as we sit under the trees lining the edge of a deserted basketball court in the South Bronx's Andrew Jackson Houses, a public housing complex in the 40th Precinct. The New York Police Department vehicles come to a screeching halt on a street corner a stone's throw from where we were sitting. A group of officers exit the wagons and begin talking to some older male residents who are casually drinking in front of an empty brick building.

Robert, a heavyset African American man who serves as the tenant association president of the Jackson Houses, races up the block to better gauge the situation. He returns a few minutes later looking troubled. Just moments earlier, the same group of men had stopped by to say hello. One of the men, David, is a close friend of Robert who is currently on parole. Robert is worried this latest arrest may translate to another bid upstate for him.

Having lived in the same apartment for his entire life, Robert has an intimate, almost encyclopedic, knowledge of the Jackson Houses that stretches back decades. In this time, he has witnessed a great deal of change in the area. The one constant, however, has been continually deteriorating conditions in the buildings he calls home. In recent years, there have been small changes to the grounds, including minor renovations to the recreation areas. But modifications have only marginally improved the quality of life. As Robert explains:

> We just had the PHAS, Public Housing Assessment Survey, that's a survey where HUD [Department of Housing and Urban Development] comes out to see how you're maintaining the building, how you're taking care of the property. How you're keeping the upkeep of people's apartments, how people are taking care of where they're renting from the government. I believe we passing, 65 is passing. We just got a 66 . . . the light fixtures in the hallways are out, and they wondering why people are getting robbed. Friday we had a gentleman get robbed, where the teenagers followed him from the store, saw the gold chain on his neck and he's coming over here where we're sitting at to sit down, until the senior citizen center opens up for lunch . . . they snatch his chain. Daylight.

In Robert's opinion, the breakdown of conditions in the Jackson Houses correlates with residents' feelings about safety. But while community members yearn for a safer neighborhood, he cautions that more aggressive policing tactics aren't the answer. Instead, he advocates a return to a form of "community policing" that existed in decades past—a theme that has consistently come up throughout my fieldwork. Robert is among many local residents who share in the collective memory of a more grounded, community-friendly police force. With the help of his mother, Ann, he recalls a time when the neighborhood's relationship with the 40th Precinct was much different:

ROBERT: There was a level of respect because the cop knew you. We had the community policing in effect. [He asks his mother, an elderly African American woman sitting with a friend on a nearby bench] What was the cop's name that used to patrol when I was younger?

ANN: It was Jesse, it was Larry, it was Phil—

ROBERT: See, and they calling first names. Jesse, Larry, Phil, Smitty . . . this was about 30 years ago, right? Thirty years ago.

ANN: 25.

ROBERT: See, we had it . . . they knew the people and they took the time. The 40th Precinct had an initiative. [Points to Ann] She's telling a story about how 25 years ago, 30 years ago, a kid ran across the street and a cop spanked the boy and took him upstairs to his mother . . . and the mother beat him. This man [the officer] walked up and down the block every day. He started to know the people. I mean, if the elderly people saw something, they said something. They felt comfortable with this man, here. Now he's not here anymore and all we got is these little knuckleheads walking up and down the street killing each other. The police come after the fact. After everybody dead, gone, bleeding. They want to come in gung ho, swinging sticks and kicking asses, and taking names later . . . and then they wanna talk about, but this is why we treat y'all like shit. Because nobody never

> wanna say nothing. Why would I want to help you solve
> a crime or tell you anything . . . and you talking to me
> like I'm a piece of trash at the bottom of your shoe?

Given the reputation the New York Police Department had during the "Bronx is Burning" 1970s, and with allegations of corruption continuing through the 1980s, it is somewhat challenging to accept these claims at face value. Nevertheless, if not an actual "return," there is something to be said about a move toward community policing.[10]

As things stand now, community-police relations are severely strained across the five boroughs. As much of my data supports, there is limited faith in the New York Police Department and in the justice system on the whole. Thus, any plan to remedy this fast deteriorating situation would have to address a massive overhaul of the current policing culture.

Although stop-and-frisk policing is often the most visible tactic used by the New York Police Department, it is only a small piece of a much larger institution that has effectively deemphasized community relations as part of sound police practice. Most precincts simply no longer (or never had) the strong community ties necessary to do good police work—to be able to differentiate between "Johnny," who works full time and attends night school, from his cousin, "Peter," who sells heroin from a park bench. Many unnecessary stops could be avoided if the beat officer had even a modicum of the knowledge countless local residents already possess. Instead, what is in place is a system that incentivizes arbitrary frisks—further distancing officers from the actual people the New York Police Department sets out to serve.

As Adrian Schoolcraft and other former officers have revealed, while the New York Police Department may not acknowledge a formal frisk quota, any form of mobility within the department may hinge on an officer's ability to make stops.[11] To that end, in 2015, a lawsuit filed by Edwin Raymond and 11 other New York Police Department officers (*Raymond et al. v. the City of New York*) alleged that officers are required to reach monthly arrest and summons goals.

Alonzo, a former officer who agreed to speak to me, spent five years working at a precinct in Midtown Manhattan. He describes the challenges of his first year on the beat:

> As far as tickets, there's a quota . . . as a rookie you come in, you need 40 summons. It could be parking summons, it could be, you stop a car, you give them a ticket summons, or it could be arrestable summons—they spit in the street, they jaywalk, they have warrants. Those are C summonses. They're all combined. You need a total of 40 summonses if you're a rookie. Per month. When you become unrookie [get seniority], it goes down to 20 summonses. How do you become unrookie? Like in Manhattan . . . first nine months you're walking by yourself. You don't have a partner. You *need* that 40 summonses.

In New York City, rookie officers are often assigned to so-called high-impact precincts. Upon taking office in January

2014, Commissioner Bratton vowed to discontinue the practice, instead opting to either pair rookies with more seasoned officers or to send them to different precincts altogether. Yet, only months into Bratton's stay, 28-year-old Akai Gurley was shot and killed by an officer in the Louis H. Pink Houses, a public housing development in the East New York section of Brooklyn. Peter Liang, an officer with less than 18 months experience, was ultimately convicted and sentenced to probation and community service—effectively evading any time behind bars.

Community relations are further jeopardized by constantly rotating personnel (officers often await a transfer to "more desirable" jurisdictions). What is perhaps most detrimental, however, is how the New York Police Department has parceled out its police force into individualized units that too often function in silos. The police force would benefit from teams of foot patrol officers who develop a rapport with a given community and are then accountable both to their unit and to the residents of that neighborhood—with an added emphasis on deescalating situations and granting second chances when possible, instead of relying on more punitive actions such as citation or arrest.

The San Diego Police Department has continually been cited for its ability to reconcile community safety with residents' rights. Experiencing a similarly dramatic crime decline throughout the 1990s, San Diego did not rely on aggressive policing tactics to achieve this. Instead, the city's program is based upon the idea that "police and citizens share responsibility for identifying and solving crime problems and that law enforcement is one important tool for addressing crime, but it is not an end in itself."[12]

In other words, the city implemented a collaborative form of policing, incentivizing *participation* in the community safety process. Whether or not this model could be effective in a complex megacity like New York, it goes a long way to shift the discussion toward community members reclaiming both their neighborhoods and their fundamental rights as citizens.

Epilogue

Kwesi and I stood quietly in front of an ice cream shop near 149th Street, a few short blocks from the epicenter of "the Hub" commercial district in the Bronx. From our location on the curb, the faint sound of sirens was being drowned out by a bass-heavy song coming from an older model Honda Accord a few feet away. Our cones hopelessly melted away in the summer heat.

As we spoke, the sweat was beginning to show through the base of his tan hat. Kwesi was feeling anxious from all of the planning and coordinating he would have to do in the upcoming days. Next week, he would be graduating from college with his bachelor's degree. Family he hadn't seen in some time would be coming in from Brooklyn and Staten Island to help him celebrate. His mother, still in citizenship limbo in Ghana, would not be able to make it.

Despite this notable milestone, Kwesi's affect seemed flat. "The free ride is over," he said under his breath. Now that he was done with school, his father would be expecting him to contribute to the monthly rent. A few weeks ago, Kwesi secured an internship at an area nonprofit that would pay him $4,000 for the summer. This, he believed, could sustain him through the early fall. "But what about after?," he wondered.

* * *

After relocating to Southern California for work a little under a year prior, I returned to the southwest Bronx in the summer of 2016. Only so much can change in a year, I told myself. And while this statement held true for the most part, there would be a number of seismic shifts in the upcoming months that would dramatically alter things in the southwest Bronx and nationally.

While critics warned that crime in New York City would surge if the NYPD were to ease its reliance on stop and frisk, the data show otherwise. Crime continued to decline in Mayor Bill De Blasio's first term as mayor, as he seemed to double down on some of his campaign promises to change the culture of the police department. In September 2016, De Blasio tapped James P. O'Neill to succeed New York Police Department commissioner William Bratton, who would step down from office. This selection was made in part due to O'Neill's commitment to "neighborhood policing," a system designed to build stronger ties between police and the community and marked by neighborhood coordination officers, or NCOs, who serve as a bridge between the community and the police force.

A little over two months after O'Neill's appointment, Donald J. Trump was elected America's 45th president. As with much of the country, in the southwest Bronx there were equal parts shock, confusion, and uncertainty. What would the ripples effects be for young people in the area? In the months leading up to the election, Trump had continually restated his firm commitment to "law and order" policing. In a September debate with Democratic presidential nominee Hillary Clinton, for example, he made a special point to acknowledge how effective he believed aggressive policing tactics had been in New York City. "Stop and frisk had a tremendous impact on the safety of New York City," he stated. "Tremendous beyond belief. So when you said it had no impact, it really did. It had a very, very big impact."[1]

In early 2017, Trump appointed Alabama senator Jeff Sessions, a politician with a history of racism accusations, as the 84th United States attorney general. Despite declining crime rates nationwide, Sessions has seemed keen on a return to the very same "tough on crime" policies that marred previous decades. Shortly after being appointed attorney general, Sessions signaled his intention to stop monitoring law enforcement agencies with histories of civil rights abuses, a move that could, of course, have huge implications for police departments in places like Ferguson, Baltimore, and New York City. At the time of this writing, no new consent decrees, legally binding agreements designed to curb police misconduct and reform departments, have been issued by the Justice Department under Trump, while existing consent decrees are subject to review under the new administration.[2] The ideals embodied by Trump and Sessions often seem diametrically opposed to the Obama-era attempts to ensure some semblance of police accountability to residents.

While local leaders and community members have begun to mobilize against many of this regime's proposed policies, it remains to be seen how effective this resistance can be.

ACKNOWLEDGMENTS

First and foremost, this manuscript is dedicated to the people whose lived experiences fill these pages. Thank you for entrusting me with your stories.

A special thank you to Philip Kasinitz, Michael Jacobson, Bill Kornblum, and Barry Glassner—my mentors in the discipline who provided me with unparalleled guidance and honest feedback from the start.

I'd also like to thank my editors, Ilene Kalish and Maryam Arain, for their care and attentiveness throughout the publishing process. Additionally, I want to acknowledge Michael Partis, Kevin Brooks, Connie Rosenblum, Will Shaw, Lauren Dewey, Jennifer Bryan, Peter Moskos, Maria Torre, Brett Stoudt, Delores Jones-Brown, Juan Battle, Jennifer Wynn, Charis Kubrin, Demond Mullins, Calvin-John Smiley, Kevin Moran, Peter Ikeler, Sarah Martucci, David Monaghan, Melanie Lorek, all of my colleagues in the California State University at Long Beach Sociology Department, and the entire Morris Justice Project for their tremendous support at the various junctures of this project.

I have been fortunate to have an incredible (global) support system of family and friends: Sita, Justin, Anneka, and Simon Feinberg, Naren Rau, Bep Dekker, Gertruud Buur, Betsy Amster, Felecia German, Robert Mitchell, Damien

Davis, Maddox Davis, Adam Braveman, Isaiah Pickens, Raymond Hutchison, Ademola Kierstedt, Daniel Guisbond, Michael White, Thijs Mientjes, Kwame Johnson, David Duncombe, Javier Vergara, Nicholas Bolt, Mathieu Saint-Louis, Treyer Mason-Gale, Dequan Howard, Daniel Hammer, and anyone else I wasn't able to fit on this page, every day you all inspire me. Your loyalty, patience, and incredible sense of humor help keep me grounded.

To my parents, Cornelia Buur and Chaitanya Haldipur—you created an environment when I was growing up that allowed me to be curious, ask questions . . . and just be silly sometimes. Thank you for always being there.

Lastly, to my brilliant and caring wife, Donna, this book is a product of your love and unwavering support.

A version of Chapter 3, "Parenting the Dispossessed: Raising the Children of 'Stop, Question, and Frisk,'" appeared in a special issue of *Race and Justice* 8 (1): 71–93.

NOTES

PREFACE

1 This is a name local residents have given the frequently occurring
   event. Though most are unclear as to why police come down
   particularly hard on Thursday afternoons, there is some suspicion
   this may be due to some combination of a change in shifts, as well as
   the neighborhood's proximity to the courthouses.

2 Rivera 2012.

INTRODUCTION

1 Jones-Brown, Gill, and Trone 2010.

2 Merton 1936.

3 Glaser and Strauss 1967.

4 Semuels 2015.

5 Williams and Kornblum 1985.

6 A pseudonym for one of the mothers on College Avenue.

7 A pop-culture reference to the borough that alludes to its history as
   being the birthplace of hip-hop.

8 Petrie 1981.

9 Small 2007.

10 Gonzalez 2004.

11 US Census Bureau 2010.

12 Jonnes 2002.

13 City of New York, Department of Planning 2013.

14 US Census Bureau, 2008–2012 American Community Survey (a).

15 US Census Bureau, 2008–2012 American Community Survey (b).

16 Wilson 1990.

17 Massey and Denton 1993.

18 See Venkatesh (2002); Brotherton and Barrios (2004); Bourgois
   (2002); and Anderson (2000).

19 Police Department, City of New York (2012, 2017).

20 White (2014); Kane and White (2013).

21 Raab 1993.

22 Bratton and Knobler 1998, 195.

23 It should be noted that crime had already begun to decline under the Dinkins administration.

24 Bratton and Knobler 1998, 198–199.

25 Wilson and Kelling 1982.

26 Estimates vary widely as to the number of stops that are not documented by police officers.

27 Conlon 2005, 13.

28 Kelly 2015, 271.

29 Under the Trespass Affidavit Program, landlords could authorize police to patrol private buildings without the consent of tenants.

30 The Black Lives Matter movement was created in response to the acquittal of George Zimmerman in the Trayvon Martin homicide case.

31 Police Department, City of New York, NYPD CompStat Unit 2016.

32 Jones-Brown et al. (2013); Jones-Brown, Gill, and Trone (2010).

33 The Fourth Amendment of the US Constitution protects against unreasonable searches and seizures by requiring probable cause before an officer can stop a citizen in a public space. In the *Terry* decision, Justice William O. Douglas issued a strongly worded dissent questioning whether the probable cause standard could even be changed without a constitutional amendment, a role outside that of the federal judiciary. "Probable cause" has been described as evidence that makes it "more likely than not" that the suspected person is involved in criminality.

34 Jones-Brown, Gill, and Trone 2010.

35 Criminal Procedure Law 140.50, effective September 1, 1971, governs all *Terry* stops in New York City.

36 See Terry v. Ohio, dissenting opinion by Justice William O. Douglas, in Ronayne (1964) and Kuh (1965).

37 Harcourt and Meares 2010.

38 Brunson and Miller 2006.

39 Alexander 2010.

40 Muhammad 2010.

41 Butler 2017.

42 Gelman, Fagan, and Kiss 2007, 1.

43 Jones-Brown et al. 2013.

44 See Glaberson 2013.

45 See Gonnerman 2014.

46 Stoudt, Fine, and Fox 2011.

47 Weber 1946, 78.

48 See Wacquant (2009) and Young (1999).

49 Anderson 2000.

50 Patillo, Weiman, and Western 2004.

51 Clear 2007.

52 LeBlanc 2003.

53 Tonry 1996.

54 Western 2007, 129.

55 Pew Center on the States 2008.

56 The right to the city, as the renowned scholar David Harvey notes, is marked by "the freedom to make and remake ourselves and our cities" (2012, 4).

57 See Whyte (1943); Liebow (1967); and Anderson (1976).

58 Jay-Z 2010, 154.

59 Lipsky 1980, 3.

60 Lipsky 1980, 11.

61 See Goffman 1959.

CHAPTER 1. THE INVISIBLE

1 Similar distinctions have been utilized in past studies. Most notably, William F. Whyte distinguished between "College Boys" and "Corner Boys" in his study of Italian immigrants in Boston, *Street Corner Society: The Social Structure of an Italian Slum* (1943).

2 DuBois 1996.

3 The area has been subject to a series of drug- and gang-related investigations, culminating in multiple indictments over the past five or more years.

4 During the summer, New York City opens up various schools and recreation centers for young adults to play basketball and other sports. In areas like the southwest Bronx, these are some of the few local outlets available to youth during the hot summer months.

5 Garcia (2003) details the evolution of the New York City sneaker culture from the 1960s through the 1980s.

6 Pattillo-McCoy (1999); May and Chaplin (2008) further elaborate on the intersection of race and clothing in different settings.

7 A puffy, down-filled winter jacket produced by Marmot. These jackets cost upwards of $500 and are highly popular among youth in the Bronx.

8 Kasinitz and Rosenberg 1996, 194.

9 Smith 2005.

10 Sammy was murdered attempting to break up a fight "Uptown" in the northern Bronx; the case garnered a significant amount of media attention.

11 A mutual associate who resides near 164th Street.

12 Rios 2011.

13 New York City School-Justice Partnership Task Force 2013.

CHAPTER 2. GROWING UP UNDER SURVEILLANCE

1 See Gottschalk (2015) for a discussion of the growth of the carceral state.

2 Police Department, City of New York 2013.

3 LaPlante, Dunn, and Carnig 2014.

4 Public Science Project 2013.

5 Justice Mapping Center 2006.

6 Justice Atlas of Sentencing and Corrections 2008.

7 ATI/Reentry Coalition 2010.

8 Measure of America of the Social Science Research Council 2012.

9 See Bushway, Stoll, and Weiman (2007); Pager (2007); Patillo, Weiman, and Western (2004); Uggen, Manza, and Thompson (2006); and Trimbur (2009).

10 N.Y. Criminal Procedure Law § 720.10—Youthful offender procedure designated for young adults ages 16–19. This is not awarded to everyone; rather, this depends heavily upon the presentence investigation of the defendant and is typically reserved for first-time offenders.

11 Tuttle and Schneider 2012.

12 See Merton 1938.

13 Garland 1993.

14 Bloomberg 2013.

15 Rosenfeld and Fornango 2014, 2017.

CHAPTER 3. PARENTING THE DISPOSSESSED

1 Comfort 2008.

2 See Brunson and Weitzer (2011) for an additional discussion on the conventions of having "the talk."

3 Riggs and Kilpatrick 1990.

4 Data suggest some of these stops may actually be repeat stops of the same person.

5 New York Civil Liberties Union 2012.

CHAPTER 4. POLICING IMMIGRANT COMMUNITIES

1 City of New York, Department of Planning 2013.

2 City of New York, Department of Planning 2013.

3 Portes and Rumbaut 2001.

4 Portes and Rumbaut 2001, 10.

5 See Mittelberg and Waters (1992) and Kasinitz et al. (2008).

6 City of New York, Department of Planning 2013.

7 City of New York, Department of Planning 2013.

8 Kasinitz et al. 2008.

9 Located in the Hunts Point section of the Bronx, this juvenile facility developed a less than desirable reputation for being particularly harsh on its juvenile detainees. It finally shut its doors in 2011.

10 Cooper 1999.

CHAPTER 5. LOSING YOUR RIGHT TO THE CITY

1 Shaw and McKay 1942.

2 Kubrin and Weitzer 2003, 374.

3 Clear 2007.

4 Sampson, Raudenbush, and Earls 1997.

5 Tyler (1988); Geller et al. (2014); Sunshine and Tyler (2003).

6 Tyler and Jackson 2013, 1.

7 Wiley and Esbensen 2013.

8 Fratello, Rengifo, and Trone 2013, 1.

9 Lipsky 2010.

10 Though presented as a popular alternative to more traditional approaches to policing, scholars like Alex Vitale (2017) and Steve Herbert (2006) argue that even this approach may simply increase the influence of police rather than empower the community itself.

11 In 2010, Schoolcraft leaked a series of recordings from Brooklyn's 81st Precinct to the *Village Voice*. The recordings revealed evidence of manipulation of statistics as well a quota system.

12 Greene 1999, 182.

EPILOGUE

1 Blake 2016.

2 Eder, Protess, and Dewan 2017.

REFERENCES

Alexander, Michelle. 2010. *The new Jim Crow: Mass incarceration in the age of colorblindness*. New York: New Press.

Anderson, Elijah. 1976. *A place on the corner*. Chicago: University of Chicago Press.

———. 2000. *Code of the street: Decency, violence, and the moral life of the inner city*. New York: W. W. Norton.

ATI/Reentry Coalition. 2010. *The New York City ATI/Reentry Coalition Services Report 2010*. New York: ATI/Reentry Coalition.

Blake, Aaron. 2016. "The first Trump-Clinton presidential debate transcript, annotated." *Washington Post*, September 26.

Bloomberg, Michael. 2013. Michael Bloomberg: "Stop and frisk' keeps New York safe. *Washington Post*, August 18.

Bourgois, Philippe. 2002. *In search of respect: Selling crack in El Barrio*. Cambridge: Cambridge University Press.

Bratton, William, and Peter Knobler. 1998. *Turnaround: How America's top cop reversed the crime epidemic*. New York: Random House.

Brotherton, David C., and Luis Barrios. 2004. *The Almighty Latin King and Queen Nation: Street politics and the transformation of a New York City gang*. New York: Columbia University Press.

Brunson, Rod K., and Jody Miller. 2006. Gender, race, and urban policing: The experience of African-American youths. *Gender & Society* 20: 531–552.

Brunson, Rod K., and Ronald Weitzer. 2009. Police relations with black and white youth in different urban neighborhoods. *Urban Affairs Review* 44 (6): 858–885.

———. 2011. Negotiating unwelcome police encounters: The intergenerational transmission of conduct norms. *Journal of Contemporary Ethnography* 40 (4): 425–456.

Bushway, Shawn, Michael A. Stoll, and David F. Weiman. 2007. *Barriers to reentry? The labor market for released prisoners in post-industrial America.* New York: Russell Sage Foundation.

Butler, Paul. 2017. *Chokehold: Policing black men.* New York: New Press.

City of New York, Department of Planning. 2013. *The newest New Yorkers: Characteristics of the city's foreign-born population, 2013 edition.* New York: City of New York.

Clear, Todd R. 2007. *Imprisoning communities: How mass incarceration makes disadvantaged neighborhoods worse.* New York: Oxford University Press.

Cloward, Richard A., and Lloyd E. Ohlin. 1960. *Delinquency and opportunity: A theory of delinquent gangs.* New York: Free Press.

Comfort, Megan. 2008. *Doing time together: Love and family in the shadow of the prison.* Chicago: University of Chicago Press.

Conlon, Edward. 2005. *Blue blood.* New York: Riverhead Books.

Contreras, Randol. 2013. *The stickup kids: Race, drugs, violence, and the American dream.* Berkeley: University of California Press.

Cooper, Michael. 1999. Officers in Bronx fire 41 shots, and an unarmed man is killed. *New York Times,* February 5, B5.

Criminal Law. New York authorizes police to "stop-and-frisk" on reasonable suspicion. N. Y. Sess. Laws 1964, ch. 86, § 2, N. Y. Code Crim. Proc. § 180(a). (1964). *Harvard Law Review* 78 (2): 473–477.

Du Bois, W. E. B. (1903) 1996. *The souls of black folk.* New York: Penguin.

Eder, Steve, Ben Protess, and Shaila Dewan. 2017. How Trump's hands-off approach to policing is frustrating some chiefs. *New York Times,* November 21, A1.

Foucault, Michel. 1979. *Discipline and punish: The birth of the prison.* New York: Vintage Books.

Fratello, Jennifer, Andres F. Rengifo, and Jennifer Trone. 2013. *Coming of age with stop and frisk: Experiences, self-perceptions, and public safety implications.* New York: Vera Institute of Justice.

Garcia, Bobbito. 2006. *Where'd you get those? New York City's sneaker culture: 1960–1987.* New York: Testify Books.

Garland, David. 1993. *Punishment and modern society: A study in social theory.* Chicago: University of Chicago Press.

Geller, Amanda, Jeffrey Fagan, Tom R. Tyler, and Bruce G. Link. 2014. Aggressive policing and the mental health of young urban men. *American Journal of Public Health* 104 (12): 2321–2327.

Gelman, Andrew, Jeffrey Fagan, and Alex Kiss. 2007. An analysis of the NYPD's stop-and-frisk policy in the context of claims of racial bias. *Journal of the American Statistical Association* 102 (479).

Glaberson, William. 2013. Faltering courts, mired in delays. *New York Times*, April 13.

Glaser, Barney G., and Anselm L. Strauss. 1967. *The discovery of grounded theory: Strategies for qualitative research*. New York: Aldine Transactions.

Goffman, Alice. 2009. On the run: Wanted men in a Philadelphia ghetto. *American Sociological Review* 74 (3): 339–357.

———. 2014. *On the run: Fugitive life in an American city*. Chicago: University of Chicago Press.

Goffman, Erving. 1959. *The presentation of self in everyday life*. New York: Doubleday Anchor Books.

Gonnerman, Jennifer. 2014. Before the law. *New Yorker*, October 6.

Gonzalez, Evelyn. 2004. *The Bronx*. New York: Columbia University Press.

Gottschalk, Marie. 2015. *Caught: The prison state and the lockdown of American politics*. Princeton, NJ: Princeton University Press.

Greene, Judith A. 1999. Zero tolerance: A case study of police policies and practices in New York City. *Crime & Delinquency* 45 (2): 171–187.

Haldipur, Jan. 2018. Parenting the dispossessed: Raising the children of "Stop, Question, and Frisk." *Race and Justice* 8 (1): 71-93.

Harcourt, Bernard E., and Tracey L. Meares. 2010. Randomization and the Fourth Amendment. *John M. Olin Law & Economics Working Paper No. 530 (2D Series); Public Law & Legal Theory Working Paper No. 317*. Chicago: University of Chicago Law School.

Harvey, David. 2012. *Rebel cities: From the right to the city to the urban revolution*. New York: Verso.

Herbert, Steve. 2006. *Citizens, cops, and power: Recognizing the limits of community*. Chicago: University of Chicago Press.

Hochschild, Arlie Russell, and Anne Machung. 1989. *The second shift: Working families and the revolution at home*. New York: Penguin Books.

Jacobson, Michael. 2006. *Downsizing prisons: How to reduce crime and end mass incarceration.* New York: New York University Press.

Jay-Z. 2010. *Decoded.* New York: Spiegel & Grau.

Jones-Brown, Delores, Jaspreet Gill, and Jennifer Trone. 2010. Stop, question & frisk policing practices in New York City: A primer. New York: John Jay College of Criminal Justice.

Jones-Brown, Delores, Brett G. Stoudt, Brian Johnston, and Kevin Moran. 2013. Stop, question & frisk policing practices in New York City: A primer (Revised). New York: John Jay College of Criminal Justice.

Jonnes, Jill. 2002. *South Bronx rising: The rise, fall, and resurrection of an American city.* New York: Fordham University Press.

Justice Atlas of Sentencing and Corrections. 2008. *Prison release rates: New York, NY.* www.justiceatlas.org.

Justice Mapping Center. 2006. *NYC Analysis.* www.justicemapping.org .

Kane, Robert J., and Michael D. White. 2013. *Jammed up: Bad cops, police misconduct, and the New York City Police Department.* New York: New York University Press.

Kasinitz, Philip, John H. Mollenkopf, Mary C. Waters, and Jennifer Holdaway. 2008. *Inheriting the city: The children of immigrants come of age.* New York: Russell Sage Foundation.

Kasinitz, Philip, and Jan Rosenberg. 1996. Missing the connection: Social isolation and employment on the Brooklyn waterfront. *Social Problems* 43 (2): 180–196.

Kelly, Raymond. 2015. *Vigilance: My life serving America and protecting its empire city.* New York: Hachette Books.

Kubrin, Charis, and Ronald Weitzer. 2003. New directions in social disorganization theory. *Journal of Research in Crime and Delinquency* 40 (4): 374–402.

Kuh, Richard H. 1965. Reflections on New York's stop-and-frisk law and its claimed unconstitutionality. *Journal of Criminal Law and Criminology* 56 (1): 32–38.

LaPlante, Sara, Christopher Dunn, and Jennifer Carnig. 2014. *Stop & frisk during the Bloomberg administration, 2002–2013.* New York: New York Civil Liberties Union.

Lardner, James, and Thomas Reppetto. 2000. *NYPD: A city and its police.* New York: Owl Books.

LeBlanc, Adrian Nicole. 2003. *Random family: Love, drugs, trouble, and coming of age in the Bronx*. New York: Scribner.

Liebow, Elliot. 1967. *Tally's corner: A study of Negro streetcorner men*. Boston: Little, Brown & Company.

Lipsky, Michael. 1980. *Street-level bureaucracy: Dilemmas of the individual in public services*. New York: Russell Sage Foundation.

Massey, Douglas S., and Nancy A. Denton. 1993. *American apartheid: Segregation and the making of the underclass*. Cambridge, MA: Harvard University Press.

May, Reuben A. Buford, and Kenneth Sean Chaplin. 2008. Cracking the code: Race, class, and access to nightclubs in urban America. *Qualitative Sociology* 31: 57–72.

Merton, Robert K. 1936. The unanticipated consequences of purposive social action. *American Sociological Review* 1 (6): 894–904.

———. 1938. Social structure and anomie. *American Sociological Review* 3: 672–782.

Mittelberg, David, and Mary C. Waters. 1992. The process of ethnogenesis among Haitian and Israeli immigrants in the United States. *Ethnic and Racial Studies* 15 (3): 412–435.

Muhammad, Khalil. 2010. *The condemnation of blackness: Race, crime, and the making of modern urban America*. Cambridge, MA: Harvard University Press.

Measure of America of the Social Science Research Council. 2012. *Youth disconnection in New York City*. Brooklyn: Social Science Research Council.

New York City School-Justice Partnership Task Force. 2013. *Keeping kids in school and out of court: Report and recommendations*. New York: New York State Permanent Judicial Commission on Justice for Children.

New York Civil Liberties Union. 2012. *Stop and frisk 2011, NYCLU briefing*. New York: NYCLU.

Pager, Devah. 2007. *Marked: Race, crime, and finding work in an era of mass incarceration*. Chicago: University of Chicago Press.

Patillo-McCoy, Mary. 1999. *Black picket fences: Privilege and peril among the black middle-class*. Chicago: University of Chicago Press.

Patillo, Mary, David Weiman, and Bruce Western. 2004. *Imprisoning America: The social effects of mass incarceration*. New York: Russell Sage Foundation.

Petrie, Daniel, director. 1981. *Fort Apache the Bronx*. Los Angeles: 20th Century Fox Film Corporation.

Pew Center on the States. 2008. *One in 100: Behind bars in America 2008*. San Francisco: Pew Charitable Trusts.

Police Department, City of New York. 2012. Crime and enforcement activity in New York City (January 1–December 31, 2011). Accessed January 4, 2018, www.nyc.gov.

———. 2013. Press release: Operation Crew Cut results. Accessed January 10, 2014, www.nyc.gov.

———. 2017. Crime and enforcement activity in New York City (January 1–December 31, 2016). Accessed June 14, 2017, www1.nyc.gov.

Police Department, City of New York, NYPD CompStat Unit. 2014. CompStat report covering the week 3/10/2014 through 3/16/2014, 44th Precinct. Vol. 21, no. 11.

Portes, Alejandro, and Ruben G. Rumbaut. 2001. *Legacies: The story of the immigrant second generation*. Berkeley: University of California Press.

Public Science Project. 2013. *The Morris Justice Project: A summary of our findings*. Accessed June 20, 2017, www.morrisjustice.org.

Raab, Selwyn. 1993. New York's police allow corruption, Mollen Panel says. *New York Times*, December 29, B2.

Riggs, David S., and Dean G. Kilpatrick. 1990. Families and friends: Indirect victimization by crime. In *Victims of crime: Problems, policies, and programs*, ed. Arthur Lurigio, Wesley Skogan, and Robert Davis, 20–138. Thousand Oaks: Sage.

Rios, Victor. 2011. *Punished: Policing the lives of black and Latino boys*. New York: New York University Press.

Rivera, Ray. 2012. Pockets of city see higher use of force during police stops. *New York Times*, August 16, A17.

Ronayne, John. 1964. The right to investigate and New York's "stop and frisk" law. 33 *Fordham Law Review* 2: 211–238.

Rosenfeld, Richard, and Robert Fornango. 2014. The impact of police stops on precinct robbery and burglary rates in New York City, 2003–2010. *Justice Quarterly* 31 (1): 96–122.

———. 2017. The relationship between crime and stop, question, and frisk rates in New York City neighborhoods. *Justice Quarterly* 34 (6): 931–951.

Rumbaut, Ruben G., and Alejandro Portes. 2001. *Ethnicities: Children of immigrants in America*. Berkeley: University of California Press.

Sampson, Robert J., Stephen W. Raudenbush, and Felton Earls. 1997. Neighborhoods and violent crime: A multilevel study of collective efficacy. *Science* 277: 918–924.

Schwirtz, Michael. 2014. New York council sees flawed mental health system. *New York Times*, March 28, A22.

Semuels, Alana. 2015. How to decimate a city. *Atlantic Monthly*. Accessed December 1, 2015, www.theatlantic.com.

Shaw, Clifford R., and Henry McKay. 1942. *Juvenile delinquency and urban areas*. Chicago: University of Chicago Press.

Small, Mario Luis. 2007. Is there such thing as "the ghetto"? The perils of assuming the South Side of Chicago represents poor black neighborhoods. *City* 11 (3): 413–421.

Smith, Sandra Susan. 2005. "Don't put my name on it": Social capital activation and job-finding assistance among the black urban poor. *American Journal of Sociology* 111 (1): 1–57.

Stoudt, Brett, Michelle Fine, and Madeline Fox. 2011. Growing up policed in the age of aggressive policing policies. *New York Law School Law Review* 56 (4): 1331–1370.

Sunshine, Jason, and Tom R. Tyler. 2003. The role of procedural justice and legitimacy in shaping public support for policing. *Law & Society Review* 37: 513–548.

Tonry, Michael. 1996. *Malign neglect: Race, crime and punishment in America*. New York: Oxford University Press.

Trimbur, Lucia. 2009. "Me and the law is not friends": How former prisoners make sense of reentry. *Qualitative Sociology* 32: 259–277.

Tuttle, Ross, and Erin Schneider. 2012. Stopped-and-frisked: "For being a f**king mutt." *Nation*. October 8. Video. www.thenation.com.

Tyler, Tom R. 1988. What is procedural justice? Criteria used by citizens to assess the fairness of legal procedures. *Law & Society Review* 22: 103–135.

Tyler, Tom R., and Jonathan Jackson. 2013. Popular legitimacy and the exercise of legal authority: Motivating compliance, cooperation, and engagement. *Psychology, Public Policy, and Law* 20 (1): 78–95.

Uggen, Christopher, Jeff Manza, and Melissa Thompson. 2006. Citizenship, democracy, and the civic reintegration of criminal offenders. *Annals of the American Academy of Political and Social Science* 605: 281–310.

US Census Bureau. 2010. *American FactFinder fact sheet: 10451, Bronx, NY*. Accessed March 7, 2014, http://factfinder2.census.gov.

———. 2008–2012 American Community Survey (a). *American FactFinder fact sheet: 10451, Bronx, NY*. Accessed March 7, 2014, http://factfinder2.census.gov.

———. 2008–2012 American Community Survey (b). *American FactFinder fact sheet: 10024, New York, NY*. Accessed March 7, 2014, factfinder2.census.gov.

Venkatesh, Sudhir Alladi. 2002. *American project: The rise and fall of a modern ghetto*. Cambridge, MA: Harvard University Press.

———. 2006. *Off the books: The underground economy of the urban poor*. Cambridge, MA: Harvard University Press.

———. 2008. *Gang leader for a day: A rogue sociologist takes to the streets*. New York: Penguin Press.

Vitale, Alex. 2017. *The end of policing*. New York: Verso.

Wacquant, Loïc. 2009. *Punishing the poor: The neoliberal government of social insecurity*. Durham, NC: Duke University Press.

Weber, Max. 1946. Politics as a vocation. In *From Max Weber: Essays in sociology*, translated by S. S. Gerth and C. Wright Mills. Oxford: Oxford University Press.

Western, Bruce. 2007. *Punishment and inequality in America*. New York: Russell Sage Foundation.

White, Michael D. 2014. The New York City Police Department, its crime control strategies and organizational changes, 1970–2009. *Justice Quarterly* 31 (1): 110–131.

Whyte, William F. (1943) 1993. *Street corner society: The social structure of an Italian slum, 4th ed.* Chicago: University of Chicago Press.

Wiley, Stephanie A., and Finn-Aage Esbensen. 2013. The effect of police contact: Does official intervention result in deviance amplification? *Crime & Delinquency* 62 (3): 283–307.

Williams, Terry, and William Kornblum. 1985. *Growing up poor*. New York: Lexington Books.

Wilson, James Q., and George L. Kelling. 1982. Broken windows: The police and neighborhood safety. *Atlantic Monthly* 249 (3): 29–37.

Wilson, William Julius. 1990. *The truly disadvantaged: The inner city, the underclass, and public policy.* Chicago: University of Chicago Press.

Young, Jock. 1999. *The exclusive society.* London: Sage Publications.

Zimring, Franklin E. 2011. *The city that became safe: New York's lessons for urban crime and its control.* New York: Oxford University Press.

INDEX

ABOUT THE AUTHOR

Jan Haldipur is Assistant Professor of Sociology at California State University, Long Beach.